高等院校"十二五"规划教材·专业基础课系列

会 计 英 语
(第 2 版)

刘智英　李　杨　徐宏幸　编　著

清华大学出版社
北京

内容简介

本书共分为四个部分、16个单元，第一部分是会计学的入门课程，介绍了会计的簿记循环，包括会计元素、会计等式、复式记账法、试算平衡表以及如何编制财务报表，帮助初学者了解和掌握西方簿记的有关知识；第二部分到第四部分分别介绍了资产、负债、所有者权益的相关知识和业务处理。全球化、知识化、人本化和信息化是21世纪的时代特征，为适应时代的要求和充分考虑21世纪财经类人才的基本知识素养，本书的每一章节都配有相应的金融管理类知识的拓展，并且有相应的习题训练，便于学生进行自测和提升。

本书可作为高等学校会计类专业的教科书，也可供金融学、管理学和其他各专业学习会计英语选用，同时可作为从事会计实务读者的参考资料。

图书在版编目(CIP)数据

会计英语/刘智英，李杨，徐宏幸编著. —2版. —北京：清华大学出版社，2019 (2025.7重印)
(高等院校"十二五"规划教材·专业基础课系列)
ISBN 978-7-302-52027-6

Ⅰ. ①会… Ⅱ. ①刘…②李… ③徐… Ⅲ. ①会计—英语—高等学校—教材 Ⅳ. ①F23

中国版本图书馆 CIP 数据核字(2019)第 005370 号

责任编辑：孟　攀
封面设计：杨玉兰
责任校对：王明明
责任印制：宋　林
出版发行：清华大学出版社
　　　　网　　　址：https://www.tup.com.cn, https://www.wqxuetang.com
　　　　地　　　址：北京清华大学学研大厦 A 座　　　邮　　编：100084
　　　　社 总 机：010-83470000　　　　　　　　　　邮　　购：010-62786544
　　　　投稿与读者服务：010-62776969, c-service@tup.tsinghua.edu.cn
　　　　质量反馈：010-62772015, zhiliang@tup.tsinghua.edu.cn
　　　　课件下载：https://www.tup.com.cn , 010-62791865
印 装 者：三河市龙大印装有限公司
经　　销：全国新华书店
开　　本：185mm×260mm　　　印　张：13.5　　　字　数：330千字
版　　次：2013 年 8 月第 1 版　2019 年 8 月第 2 版　印　次：2025 年 7 月第 5 次印刷
定　　价：39.00 元

产品编号：079165-01

第 2 版前言

随着我国国际化进程的加快，英语能力已成为衡量当今财务人员是否合格的一个重要标准。作为 21 世纪的会计专业的精英，其职责已不再是单纯的数据记录、分类和汇总，更重要的是进行经济现象分析，并参与企业经营管理。这就要求财经类毕业生具有较强的沟通能力，包括用英语进行沟通的能力。为此，编者根据长期的教学和实践经验对本书进行了再编。

本书具有如下几个方面的特点。

内容系统：本书的内容具有很强的系统性。第一部分介绍会计簿记、会计等式、复式记账法等基本知识，探讨会计循环的各个环节。第二部分介绍了资产，包括现金、银行调节表、库存、应收账款、固定资产以及无形资产等相关业务。第三部分介绍了负债，包括应付账款、应付债券等相关内容。第四部分介绍了所有者权益，包括合伙制企业以及股份有限公司。本书没有采用此类书籍以阅读方式为主的传统做法，而是采用基本知识、补充资料和常用词句相结合的编写方式，使教材看起来更为生动。

实用性强：会计是一个技术性较强的行业，所以编者在概念的解释、方法的讲解等方面特别注意实用性和可操作性。对于理论知识的介绍，本书尤其注重与实务相结合，因此本书选取了丰富的范例，帮助读者在学习会计专业英语的同时掌握实用的会计知识。

本书具体分工如下：哈尔滨金融学院刘智英老师负责第一单元到第六单元，哈尔滨金融学院李杨老师负责第七单元到第十一单元，哈尔滨金融学院徐宏幸老师负责第十二单元到第十六单元。本书由刘智英老师统纂全稿，张铁军老师对本书进行了审核。

在编写过程中，编者在选材和编写方式上做了一些新的尝试，希望能取得良好的效果。但教材建设是一项庞大的系统工程，任何一项改革都不是一蹴而就的，或多或少都会存在一些不尽如人意之处，需要不断改进和完善。恳请广大读者对本教材的不足之处多提宝贵的意见。

编 者

第 1 版前言

在当今全球经济一体化的大背景下，社会的人才观正在发生着巨大的变化——由单一型的专门人才向复合型人才转变。各行各业的从业人员不但要精通业务知识，还要掌握相关的专业英语，这样才能有效地学习与专业知识相关的英文资料，处理好涉外事务。专业英语教学对于学生掌握职业技能、形成综合职业能力以及后续学习和发展都具有重要的作用。作为专业英语的一个组成部分，会计英语的重要性也日益显现。

会计英语的教学涉及会计教育的改革，教材是教育改革的重要基础环节，没有优秀的教材就无法培养出优秀的学生。为了使高等学校学生以及广大会计实务工作者更好地掌握会计专业知识，加强英语语言与会计专业之间的整体联系，从而在英语中体会和理解会计理论，在会计场景中学习和掌握英语，达到能够熟练阅读英文会计文献和使用英语处理会计事务的目的，我们特地编写了本教材，以满足培养高素质会计人才的需要。本教材全面而系统地反映了现代会计最新的发展水平和趋势，融合了西方会计学理论，能适应信息化社会中对知识学习、更新和积累的需要。

作者长期从事会计基础和会计英语教学，在教学实践中积累了丰富的经验和翔实的材料，写作中注重简单、实用，多用案例来说明问题。

本教材的主要特色如下。

(1) 在体例上，避免使用传统的大块文章做课文，力求言简意赅，通俗易懂。

(2) 在材料的选择上，本书强调范例的多样性，同时给学生提供充实的综合能力训练。

(3) 在内容上，切实与学生的实际水平相符，紧跟会计专业发展的最新动态，既容易理解，又反映前沿的成果。

(4) 专业词汇涉及面广，不仅涵盖了会计专业知识，也涉及金融及电子商务等方面的专业词汇，开阔了学生的视野。

本书涉及会计学中最基本的原理、原则，涵盖了会计专业常用的词汇，牵涉到了实际业务操作方面的内容；语言表述通俗、流畅，基本原理、术语、概念表述准确；体例设计的独特性容易引起读者兴趣，注重对学生思维的诱导和启发，能引导学生积极参与到课堂教学中。为了防止在教学过程中学生有了中文翻译便不注意听讲现象的发生，本书尽量减少中文，力求以大量简洁明快的英文来诠释会计专业知识。

本教材共分三个部分：第一部分介绍了会计学的基本理论和体系，第二部分重点介绍了经济业务的流程处理，第三部分介绍了调整事项和财务会计报表的初步知识。

本书由刘智英老师主编，由张铁军负责审核，李杨和徐宏幸老师参与了本书的编写。

在编写本教材时，在体例和选材上做了一些新的尝试，希望能取得良好的效果。但教材建设是一项庞大的系统工程，任何一项改革都不是一蹴而就的，都或多或少存在一些不尽如人意之处，需要不断修改和完善。我们恳请广大读者对本教材的不足之处多提宝贵的意见。

编　者

目　　录

Part One　Bookkeeping Cycle

Part Two　　Special Topics of Assets

Part Four   Special Topics of   Owners' Equity

Part One

Part One

Chapter 1　Introduction to Accounting

After studying this chapter, you should be able to:

- Understand concepts of accounting;
- Know financial accounting and managerial accounting;
- Identify types of business entity and accounting profession;
- Grasp accounting principles.

1.1　Concepts of Accounting

Accounting is a set of concepts and techniques that are used to measure and report financial information about an economic unit. The economic unit is generally considered to be a separate enterprise. The information is potentially reported to a variety of different types of interested enterprise. Accounting is often called the "language of business". It uses its own special words and symbols to communicate financial information that is supposed to be useful for economic decision making by managers, shareholders, creditors, governmental units, financial analysts, etc. These interested parties tend to be concerned about their own interests in the entity. For example, managers need accounting information to set goals, evaluate the progress toward those goals and take corrective action; creditors are always concerned about the enterprise's ability to perform its obligations; governmental units need information to tax and regulate; financial analysts use accounting data to form their opinions on which they base their investment recommendations. Accounting is an information system of interpreting, recording, measuring, classifying, summarizing, reporting and describing business economic activities with monetary unit as its main criterion.

1.2　Financial Accounting and Managerial Accounting

Users of accounting information are a diverse group that can be divided into external users and internal users. This distinction allows us to classify accounting into two fields—financial accounting and managerial accounting.

1.2.1　Financial Accounting

Financial accounting is concerned with reporting information to external users to an entity in order to help them to make sound economic decisions about the entity's performance and financial position. These external users can not control the actual preparation of reports or have access to underlying details. Their ability to understand and their confidence in reports directly depend on standardization of the principles and practices that are used to prepare the reports. In China, a governmental department, the Ministry of Finance (MOF), is primarily responsible for setting rules that form the foundation of financial reporting. With the development of global trade, the International Accounting Standards Board(IASB) has been steadily gaining prominence as a global accounting rule setter. Financial reports prepared under the generally accepted accounting principles (GAAP) promulgated by such standard setting bodies are intended to be general purpose in orientation.

1.2.2 Managerial Accounting

Managerial accounting is about providing information to help managers run their businesses. Unlike financial accounting, managerial accounting is a separate type of accounting activity. Business managers are charged with business planning, controlling, and critical decision-making, so they may desire specialized reports, budgets, detailed product costing information, and other details that are generally not reported on an external basis. Managerial accounting is carried out by managerial accountants who need to have special abilities. Managerial accounting is used in all forms of organizations—profit-seeking and not-for-profit businesses; sole traders, partnerships and companies; retailing, manufacturing and service business, and government.

1.3 Types of Business Entity and Accounting Profession

It is necessary to know the entity and its basic business processes, and to understand the accounting profession.

1.3.1 Types of Business Entity

Businesses range enormously in size and most types of business can be classified in terms of who is involved in them and how the organizations operate. Three different types are as shown in Figure 1-1.

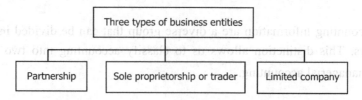

Figure 1-1　Three Types of Business Entities

Sole proprietorship or trader. An individual can run his or her own business, either alone as a one-person operation or as a business owned with several employees. The owner is entitled to all the profits and suffers all the losses from the business.

Partnership. Two or more people working together with the idea of generating profits from a business are known as partners. It is also known as firms. Partners share profits and losses in accordance with their agreements.

Limited company. This is a very common type of business because it offers the benefit of limited liability. The investment of the investors is limited to their shareholding. This is not the same in sole trader or partnership businesses where the owners may have to make up for business losses with their personal resources.

1.3.2 Procedure of Business Transaction

Every business buys goods or services from suppliers and pays for what it buys. Every business sells goods or services to customers and gets paid for what it sells. So we can say purchases and sales are the main procedures of business transaction, of course there are also other procedures. The procedure of the business is as shown in Figure 1-2.

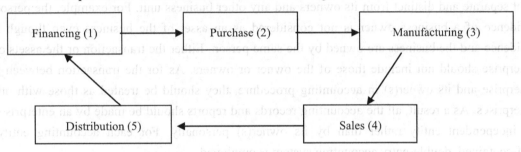

Figure 1-2　Procedure of Business Transaction

1.3.3 Accounting Profession

The rapid development of accounting in current century brings about large number of professionally trained accountants. There are several special areas in the field of accounting. Two general classifications are public accounting and private accounting. Private accountants work for a single business such as a local department store, educational institution, government agency and so on. They may focus on internal auditing, which involves reviewing the controls and procedures in use by their employers. Objectives of these reviews are to safeguard company resources and assess the reliability and accuracy of accounting information and accounting system. Public accountants are those who provide audit, tax and consulting services to the general public. Public accountants usually need to be licensed as a CPA (Certified Public Accountant). Public accounting firms are called CA firms, CPA firms, or CMA firms. The largest firms are worldwide partnerships with over 2,000 partners. The four largest accounting firms in the world are often called *the Big Four*.

Professional ethics has been a prominent and sensitive issue in the accounting profession for years. Professional accountants should obey some basic ethical standards, and the key ones are legality, integrity, objectivity, confidentiality, and competence.

1.4 Accounting Principles

Financial accounting practice is governed by concepts and rules known as generally accepted accounting principles(GAAP). These principles are not only the basic rules for identifying and measuring economic transaction, but also the guidelines for generating financial statements. Accounting principles can be introduced as the following.

1.4.1 Accounting Entity Principle

Accounting entity refers to accounting space, namely a special unit or organization, on which accounting practice and supervision are conducted. The activity of a business (enterprise) can be kept separate and distinct from its owners and any other business unit. For example, the personal residence of a business owner is not considered as an asset of the business even though the residence and the business are owned by the same person. Either the transaction or the assets of a enterprise should not include those of the owner or owners. As for the transaction between the enterprise and its owner(s) in accounting procedure, they should be treated as those with other enterprises. As a result, all the accounting records and reports should be made by an enterprise as an independent entity rather than by its owner(s) personally. For each accounting entity a self-contained, double-entry accounting system is employed.

1.4.2 Going-Concern Principle

The going-concern principle means that accounting information reflects an assumption that the business will continue operating instead of being closed or sold. This implies that property is reported at cost instead of liquidation values that assume closure. The assets used in carrying on its operations are not for sale, their current market values are not relevant and need not to be shown. However, if a business concern is about to be sold or liquidated, the going-concern principle will not be available in financial statements.

1.4.3 Accounting Period Principle

This principle is also known as the time-period principle. It is contemporary accounting practice to measure the result of an entity's operation over a relatively short period and to present a balance sheet at frequent interval. The economic activities of an enterprise can be divided into artificial time periods of equal length. The most common periods regulated in *Chinese Accounting Standards System for Business Enterprise*, are monthly, quarterly, half-yearly and yearly. The most basic accounting period is one year, and virtually all businesses prepare annual financial statements. However, a series of monthly statements often can be combined for quarterly and semiannual periods. Accountants must conduct accounting and prepare financial report periodically to provide financial information, so that all users can make their decisions based upon the information.

1.4.4   Monetary Unit Principle

Accounting is based on the assumption that money is the common denominator in business by which economic activity is conducted. The monetary unit provides an appropriate basis for accounting measurement and analysis. Examples of the monetary unit are the dollar in the United States, Canada, Australia, and Singapore; the pound sterling in United Kingdom; peso in Mexico; and Renminbi in China. However, in general, financial statements are presented in the currency of the country where the reports are published. The use of money as the unit of account does create some difficulties: transaction may not have an obvious amount in some cases and the value of the money changes over time.

1.4.5   Historical Cost Principle

This principle means that accounts should reflect the actual cost that happens in a business transaction historically. GAAP requires that companies account for and report most assets and liabilities on the basis of acquisition price. This is often referred to as the historical cost principle. Cost has an important advantage over other valuations—it emphasizes reliability. The historical cost provides users with a reliable benchmark for measuring historical trends.

1.4.6   The Consistent Principle

This principle implies that accounting methods should be consistent from one period to another, and should not be changed arbitrarily. This principle does not mean that accounting methods cannot be changed and does not require a inter-firm consistency in accounting procedures. The principle only requires that if accountings procedure are changed, the fact of the change and its effect on reported results are supposed to be disclosed in financial statements.

1.4.7   The Conservatism Principle

This principle suggests that accountants should be conservative and choose the solution that will be least likely to over state assets and income. It is a characteristic of contemporary accounting that accountants act conservatively in the measurement of profit. In general, this means that accountants use "reasonable pessimism" in measuring revenues and expenses. Revenues are not recorded until they are reasonably certain, but expenses are recorded as soon as they become probable. Similarly, when accountants have a choice of measurements of cost for assets and liabilities. The effect of this principle is that reported profits and net assets will be lower than those under most alternative assumptions.

1.4.8 The Objectivity Principle

This principle requires that accounting records and statements be based on the most accurate and reliable data. The accountant should avoid incorporating guesses or estimates in the accounting and reports. In practical terms, objectivity means that an accountant requires evidence of the existence and the amount of a transaction before recording it in the book. For many transactions the evidence is documentary, such as invoices, receipts, cash register tapes and credit notes. The documentary evidence is the stimulus for recording transaction.

Key Words and Phrases

accounting	会计
bookkeeping	簿记
financial analyst	财务分析师
financial position	财务状况
interested parties	利益相关方
financial accounting	财务会计
managerial accounting	管理会计
MOF(Ministry of Finance)	财政部
IASB(International Accounting Standards Board)	国际会计准则理事会
GAAP(Generally Accepted Accounting Principles)	一般公认会计准则
CPA(Certified Public Accountant)	注册会计师
CMA(Certified Management Accountant)	注册管理会计师
business entity	会计实体
accountant	会计人员
a sole proprietorship	独资、个体企业
a partnership	合伙企业
limited company	有限公司
financing	融资
distribution	分销
accounting profession	会计职业
internal audit	内部审计
public accountants	公共会计
private accountants	专任会计
the Big Four	国际四大会计师事务所

professional ethics	职业道德
accounting principles	会计原则
accounting entity	会计主体
double-entry accounting system	复式记账系统
going-concern	持续经营
accounting period	会计分期
monetary unit	货币计量单位
financial statement	财务报表
historical cost	历史成本
acquisition price	取得成本
consistent	一致性
disclose	披露
accounting procedures	会计程序
conservatism	谨慎
revenue	收入
objectivity	客观性

Exercises

I. Answer the following questions.

1. What is accounting?
2. What is the difference between financial accounting and managerial accounting?
3. Describe the classification of accounting profession.
4. List out different types of business entity.
5. Interpret the accounting principles.

II. Choose the best answer for each of the following statements.

1. Which of the following users are not external users of accounting information? _____.
   A. Manager   B. Creditor   C. Investor   D. Employees
2. Accounting is an information system that_____.
   A. measures business activities
   B. processes information into reports
   C. communicates financial information to decision-makers
   D. all of the above
3. Two general classifications of accounting are_____.
   A. private accounting and CPA   B. public accounting and private accounting
   C. CA and CMA   D. public accounting and managerial accounting
4. _____serves the needs of the management inside the business.

A. Private accounting   B. Government accounting

C. Public accounting   D. Managerial accounting

5. _____ are/is the basic ethics for an account.

A. Legality   B. Integrity   C. Competence   D. All of the above

6. The reports of financial accounting is based on _____.

A. management responsibility   B. double-entry system

C. decision analysis   D. internal service

7. The _____ concept holds that the entity will remain in operation for the foreseeable future.

A. going concern   B. accounting entity

C. monetary unit   D. accounting period

8. The _____ principle assures that the accounting information is reported at regular intervals.

A. going concern   B. accounting period

C. accounting entity   D. monetary unit

III. Decide whether each statement is true or false.

1. Accounting is a set of concepts and techniques that are used to measure and report financial information about a legal unit. (   )

2. Business managers need accounting information to make sound leadership decision. (   )

3. A sole proprietorship is an enterprise owned by one person. It is common for service business. (   )

4. Managerial accounting is primarily concerned with providing information to parties outside the firm. (   )

5. Financial statements are presented in the currency of the country where the reports are published. (   )

6. In accounting, all kinds of business are not treated as a separate entity. (   )

7. If accounting's procedure is changed, the fact of the change and its effect on reported results are supposed to be disclosed in the financial statements. (   )

8. The effect of the conservatism principle is that reported profits and net assets will be higher than those under most alternative assumptions. (   )

IV. Translate the following sentences into Chinese.

1. Accounting is a set of concepts and techniques that are used to measure and report financial information about an economic unit.

2. With the development of global trade, the International Accounting Standards Board (IASB) has been steadily gaining prominence as a global accounting rule setter.

Reading Materials

The Big Four

The Big Four are the four largest professional services networks in the world, offering audit, assurance services, taxation, management consulting, advisory, actuarial, corporate finance and legal services. They handle the vast majority of audits for publicly traded companies as well as many private companies. It is reported that the Big Four audit 99% of the companies in the FTSE 100, and 96% of the companies in the FTSE 250 Index, an index of the leading mid-cap listing companies. This group was once known as the "Big Eight", and was reduced to the "Big Six" and then "Big Five" by a series of mergers. The Big Five became the Big Four after the fall of Arthur Andersen in 2002, following its involvement in the Enron scandal.

1. Deloitte Touche Tohmatsu

Deloitte Touche Tohmatsu Limited commonly referred to as Deloitte, is a UK-incorporated multinational professional services firm with operational headquarters in New York City in the United States. Deloitte is one of the "Big Four" accounting firms and the largest professional services network in the world by revenue and number of professionals. Deloitte provides audit, tax, consulting, enterprise risk and financial advisory services with more than 244,400 professionals globally. In FY 2016, the company earned a record $36.8 billion USD in revenues. As of 2016, Deloitte is the 6th-largest privately owned organization in the United States. As per reports in 2012, Deloitte had the largest number of clients amongst FTSE 250 companies in the UK and in 2015, Deloitte currently has the highest market share in auditing among the top 500 companies in India. Deloitte has been ranked number one by market share in consulting by Gartner, and for the fourth consecutive year, Kennedy Consulting Research and Advisory ranks Deloitte number one in both global consulting and management consulting based on aggregate revenues. In 2016, *Fortune* magazine ranked Deloitte as one of the 100 Best Companies to Work For and *Bloomberg Business* has consistently named Deloitte as the best place to launch a career.

2. Pricewaterhouse Coopers

PwC is a global professional services firm headquartered in London, United Kingdom. With a combined headcount of more than 161,000 staff in 757 cities accross 154 countries, PwC firms rank the world's second-largest professional services firm. Aggregated revenues in fiscal year 2010 were $26.569 billion, including expenses reimbursed by clients. Their member firms performed services for 83% of the companies in the Fortune Global 500.

3. Ernst & Young

EY is the third largest professional services organization in the world with member firms in more than 140 countries, headquartered in London, UK. It employs over 140,000 staff and had total revenues of $21.255 billion in 2010. The members of the Ernst&Young global organization help companies in businesses across all industries—from emerging growth companies to global powerhouses—deal with a broad range of business issues. Ernst&Young provides a range of services, including accounting and auditing, tax reporting and operations, tax advisory.

4. KPMG

KPMG is one of professional services organization in the world. Its global headquarter is located in Amstelveen, Netherland. With around 138,000 staff working in member firms in 148 countries, they had total revenues of $20.630 billion in 2010. Their purpose is to turn knowledge into value for the benefit of their clients, their people, and the capital markets. They play an important role in the capital markets and are highly active in supporting positive reform within their industry to strengthen credibility and confidence.

Chapter 2   Accounting Elements and Accounting Equation

After studying this chapter, you should be able to:

- Distinguish cash basis and accrual basis;
- Describe accounting elements ;
- Understand accounting equations .

We will discuss the accounting elements and accounting equation but at first, we should understand the basic foundation, that is, the accounting is based on the accrual principle. There is another basic, cash basic, which is used in non-making profit business.

There are three basic financial statements which are the end products of financial accounting: balance sheet, income statement and the statement of cash flows. The nature and formats of the first two statements will be illustrated in this chapter. Balance sheet and income statement are prepared at least yearly, but it is also customary to prepare them quarterly or monthly. There are three elements to represent the balance sheet, i.e., asset, liability and owner's equity. Income, expenses and profit can represent the income statement which is the operation result of the business.

Elements of financial statements are the building blocks with which financial statements are constructed. The items in financial statements represent certain entity resources in words and numbers, claims to those resources, and the effects of transactions and other events and circumstances that result in changes in those resources and claims. So the elements are also called the items of financial accounting.

2.1   The Accounting Bases

The accrual basis and the cash basis are bases and basic ways to do accounting. Generally accepted accounting principles require that a business use the accrual basis and identify the revenues and expenses when its actual rights and liabilities incurred, which means that the business should record revenues as they are earned and expenses as they are incurred, not considering whether the cash is actually received or paid.

2.1.1   Cash Basis

In cash-basis accounting, the accountant records a transaction only when cash is received or paid. Cash receipts are treated as revenues and payments are handled as expenses. It ignores receivables, payables and depreciation. Only some small businesses use the cash basis. According to this method, revenues and expenses are recorded in the income statement during the period in which cash is received or paid. The net income is the difference between the cash receipts (revenues) and the cash payments (expenses). The income recorded on the cash basis thus could not provide a realistic picture of the company's operation.

2.1.2   Accrual Basis

Accrual-basis accounting is more complex and more competent than cash-basis accounting. In accrual-basis accounting, an accountant recognizes the impact of a business transaction as it occurs. When the business performs a service, makes a sale, or incurs an expense, the accountant records the transaction, whether or not cash has been received or paid. On the accrual basis, revenues are recorded in the income statement in the period in which they are earned. Accrual-basis accounting records cash transactions, including the following:

1. Collecting cash from customers

- Receiving cash from interest earned;
- Paying salaries, rent, income tax and other expenses;
- Borrowing money;
- Paying off loans;
- Issuing stock.

2. Recording non-cash transactions

- Purchase of inventory on account;
- Sales on account;
- Accrual of interest and other expenses incurred but not yet paid;
- Depreciation expense;
- Usage of prepaid insurance, supplies, and other prepaid expenses.

The accrual-basis accounting is designed to avoid misleading income statement results that could result from the timing of cash receipts and payments. It is often necessary to adjust some account balances at the end of each accounting period to achieve a proper matching of costs and expenses with revenues. The adjusting step occurs after the journals have been posted, but before financial statements are prepared.

2.2   Accounting Elements

Accounting elements are basic classification of accounting objects, naming those specific objects correctly. In China, there are basic kinds of accounting elements in every enterprise including assets, liabilities, owner's equity, revenue, expenses and profits. The first three elements represent the essential units of the entity's financial conditions, which are known as the elements of balance sheet. The last three elements reflect the units of the entity's operating results or business outcomes, which are called elements of the income statement. The concepts of accounting element are as below.

1. Assets

Assets are resources of an entity. It refers to the resources which result from the past transactions and events, controlled or owned by the entity, and probably bring future economic benefit to the entity.

Assets can be subdivided into current assets and non-current assets according to the time span. In another word, it is based on one operating cycle, for example, office supplies, merchandise, furniture, land, cash and so on.

Probable future economic benefits can be obtained or controlled by a particular entity as a result of past transactions or events. It results in potential future economic benefits coming into a company. Its ownership belongs to the company or it is controlled by a company. Current assets consist of cash, bank saving, inventory, account receivable, and note receivable. Non-current assets consist of fixed assets, intangible assets, and long-term investment.

2. Liability

Liabilities are "outsider claims". It's a future sacrifice of economic benefits arising from present obligations of an entity as a result of the past transactions or events. These outside parties are called creditors. For example, a creditor who has loaned money to a business has a claim—a legal right—to a part of the assets until the business pays the debts. It results in the outflow of economic benefits. The payment of liabilities is through transferring assets or providing services to other entities. The liabilities are from past transactions. Liability can be divided into current liability and non-current liability. Current liability consists of short-term loans, notes payable, accounts payable, tax payable, and wages payable, interest payable. Non-current liability has long-term loans, mortgage, and bonds payable.

3. Owners' equity

Owners' equity is called "insider claims". These are the claims held by the owners of the business. An owner has a claim to the entity's assets because he or she has invested in the business. So, it refers to the ownership interest in a corporation in the form of common stock or preferred stock. It also refers to total assets minus total liabilities, in which case it is also referred to as shareholder's equity, net worth or book value. In another word, it is the difference between what a property is worth and what the owner owes against that property. Owner's equity increases with revenue, and decreases because of expenses or an owner's withdrawal.

Owners' equity consists of the following items:

(1) Capital introduced or paid in capital: the assets introduced by owner into the company;

(2) Surplus reserve: the section from profit for future losses;

(3) Capital reserve: the income from contribution and non-monetary transactions and etc.;

(4) Undistributed profit: profit remaining after distribution.

4. Revenue

Purchase and sale are normal activities of a business, in order to earn income. Income from selling goods or services is usually called sales revenue. There might be other sources of income too, such as interest earned.

Revenue is the inflows or other enhancements of assets of an entity or settlement of its liabilities during a period from delivering or producing goods, rendering services, or other activities that constitute the entity's ongoing major or central operations.

There are three characteristics of revenue, as follows:

(1) Resulting from normal operation;

(2) Resulting in the inflow of economic benefit other than the contribution from participants;

(3) Resulting in the increases in equity ultimately.

5. Expenses

In order to earn income, a business incurs expenditure. Items of expenditure are called expenses. Expenses are the outflow of a particular entity during the accounting period which results in the decreases in equity other than the distribution to the owners.

(1) Characteristics of expenses are as follows:

- Resulting from the past transactions;
- Resulting in the outflow of economic benefit other than the distribution to the participants;
- Resulting in the decreases in equity;
- The result of outflow will result in the depletions of assets and incurrence of liabilities.

(2) Examples of expenses include the following:

- Salaries and wages for employees;
- Telephone charges and postage costs;
- The rental cost on a building used by the business;
- The interest cost on a bank loan.

6. Profit

It is the operating result for a period. There are different terms in profit such as gross profit, income from operation, income before income tax, and net income. When a business makes a profit from trading, the profit becomes a part of the owner's capital, and so is added to the capital. Profit consists of the difference between revenue and expenses, gains and losses.

Gains refer to the increases in equity from incidental events or peripheral events and from all other transactions and events, and circumstances affecting the entity during a period except those result from revenues or investments by owners. Losses refer to decreases in equity from incidental events or peripheral events of an entity and from all other transactions, events, and circumstances affecting the entity during a period except those result from expenses or distributions to owners.

Suppose there is a corporation called TIANZUO, and the owner of the business is Mr. Liu, on his first day of trading, he uses up 500 yuan of his stock, and makes sales totaling 750 yuan. All the transactions are carried out in cash. In other words, he makes 250 yuan profit on the day from trading. Profit becomes a part of the owner's capital, so the accounting equation at the end of the day will be:

The beginning equation:

Assets		Liabilities		Capital	
Equipment	2,000				
Furniture	1,500				
Table ware	800				
Stock	700				
Cash	2,000	Loan	4,000	Contributed Capital	3,000
Total	7,000		4,000		3,000

The accounting equation at the end of the day will be:

Assets		Liabilities		Capital	
Equipment	2,000				
Furniture	1,500				
Table ware	800				
Stock(700-500)	200			Contributed Capital	3,000
Cash (2000+750)	2,750	Loan	4,000	Profit	250
Total	7,250		4,000		3,250

2.3 The Calculation Method for Accounting

There are seven steps of the calculation method for accounting, as follows:
- Setting up accounting items and accounts;
- Double-entry bookkeeping;
- Making and auditing accounting documentations ;
- Registering journal and ledgers;
- Cost calculations;
- Verification of assets;
- Working out financial statements / establishment of financial statements.

2.4 Accounting Equation

2.4.1 The Content of Accounting Equation

The most basic tool of accountant is the accounting equation. Accounting equation is also called accounting formula of equilibrium which represents the basic relationship between various accounting essences. Accounting equation is used to present accounting elements and their increases and decreases. The financial statements, as the financial product of the accounting process, are prepared based on the equation. Account design，double-entry accounting and trial balance are also on the basis of this theory.

Firstly, we will introduce the balance sheet.

Accounting equation 1: **Assets = Liabilities + Owners' Equity**

This is the basic accounting equation. It shows that the assets of the business and the claims to those assets. The relationship between assets and the claims against the assets can be summarized in the following equation: assets = claims. We can say the assets are representation and the claims are sources of the assets. Claims to those assets come from two sources: outside claims and inside claims. Liabilities are outside claims, and owner's equities are inside claims. The accounting equation should remain in balance at all times because of double–entry accounting or bookkeeping. (Double-entry means that every transaction will affect two accounts in the general ledger.)

Suppose you run a business that supplies meat to fast-food restaurants. Some customers may pay you in cash when you deliver the meat. Cash is an asset. Other customers may buy on credit and promise to pay you within certain time after delivery. This promise is also an asset because it is an economic resource that will benefit you in the future when you receive cash from customer. This promise is called an account receivable. If the promise that entitles you to receive cash in the future is written out, it is called a note receivable. All receivables are assets. For example, the fast-food restaurant's promise to pay in the future for the meat it purchases on credit creates a debt for the restaurant. This liability is an account payable, which means the debtor (restaurant) usually does not give the creditor (meat seller) a written promise to pay. Instead it is backed up by the reputation and credit standing of the restaurant and its owner. A written promise of future payment is called a note payable. All payables are liabilities.

Secondly, we refer to the income statement.

Accounting equation 2: **Revenues − Expenses = Profit**

The subject or aim for the operation of the business is to obtain profit which is also called operating result. In the operation of assets, we obtain revenue in different ways matching with the expenses at the same time. Revenue is compared with the expenses and the difference is profit called operating result.

2.4.2　The Effects of Economic Transactions on the Accounting Equation

Every transaction affects at least two items in the accounting equation. The accounting equation remains in balance after each transaction.

- Assets increasing　　　　　　　claims increasing

  liability increasing or capital increasing

- Assets decreasing　　　　　　　claims decreasing

  liability decreasing or capital decreasing

- The internal changes of assets　　one asset increasing, another asset decreasing
- The internal changes about the claims

There are also four classifications about it and they are as follows:

Liability increasing	liability decreases
Capital increasing	capital decreasing
Liability increasing	capital decreasing
Capital increasing	liability decreasing

In general, there are many complex transactions in the operation but they will not destroy the equilibrium of the accounting equation. There are two situations after the changes:

(1)　The relationship about assets and equity is the same as the original equation;

(2)　The relationship about assets and equity is different from the original equation and it is a new equation.

【Example 2.1】 Giving application and analyzing the equilibrium of the equation.

On February 5, Wang Hong sets up a business by herself, trading as "Limei Toggery".

a. On that day, she invests 20,000 yuan in the company.

b. The second day she borrows 50,000 yuan from a bank for a period of 2 years.

c. On February 8, she buys into 20 pieces of clothing, costing 3,000 yuan on credit within 30 days.

d. On February 9, she sells 10 pieces of clothing totaled 2,500 yuan which is deposited in bank, the original cost for about 1,600 yuan.

e. On February 10, she sells 5 pieces of clothing totaled 1,500 yuan in cash, the original cost for about 700 yuan.

f. Feeling well pleased, she takes 500 yuan for her personal use from the company's cash tin.

g. On February 11, she writes a cheque 1,000 yuan to her supplier in part payment for the initial inventory of clothing.

Table 2-1 shows what happens to the accounting equation as each of these transactions takes place and concludes the rule.

Table 2-1　Effects of Economic Transactions on the Accounting Equation

Assets				Liabilities				Capital			
Item	Ori	CH	EB	Item	Ori	CH	EB	Item	Ori	CH	EB
Bank	20,000							Capital	20,000		

Assets				Liabilities				Capital			
Item	Ori	CH	EB	Item	Ori	CH	EB	Item	Ori	CH	EB
Bank	20,000	50,000	70,000	Long-term	50,000			Capital	20,000		

Item	Ori	CH	EB	Item	Original	CH	EB	Item	Ori	CH	EB
Bank			70,000	Long-term	50,000			Capital	20,000		
Inventory	3,000		3,000	Payables	3,000						
Total	3,000		73,000	Total	53,000			Total	20,000		

Item	Ori	CH	EB	Item	Ori	CH	EB	Item	Original	CH	EB
Bank	70,000	2,500	72,500	Long-term	50,000			Capital	20,000	900	
Inventory	3,000	-1,600	1,400	Payables	3,000						
Total	73,000	900	73,900	Total	53,000			Total	20,000	900	20,900

Item	Ori	CH	EB	Item	Ori	CH	EB	Item	Ori	CH	EB
Bank	72,500		72,500	Long-term	50,000			Capital	20,900	800	21,700
Cash	1,500		1,500								
Inventory	1,400	-700	700	Payables	3,000						
Total			74,700	Total	53,000			Total			21,700

Item	Ori	CH	EB	Item	Ori	CH	EB	Item	Ori	CH	EB
Bank	72,500		72,500	Long-term	50,000			Capital	21,700		21,700
Cash	1,500	-500	1,000					Drawing			500
Inventory	700		700	Payables	3,000						
Total	74,700	-500	74,200	Total	53,000			Total			21,200

Item	Ori	CH	EB	Item	Ori	CH	EB	Item	Ori	CH	EB
Bank	72,500	-1,000	71,500	Long-term	50,000		50,000	Capital	21,700		21,700
Cash	1,000							Drawing			500
Inventory	700		700	Payables	3,000	-1000	2,000				
Total	74,200	-1,000	73,200	Total	53,000	-1000	52,000	Total			21,200

Key Words and Phrases

accounting elements	会计要素
accounting equation	会计等式
accounting bases	会计核算基础
cash-basis	现金收付制
accrual-basis	权责发生制
balance sheet	资产负债表
income statement	利润表
financial statement	财务报表
inventory	存货，详细目录
receivables	应收账款
payables	应付账款
depreciation	贬值
assets	资产
liability	负债
owner's equity	所有者权益
revenue	收入
expenses	费用
gains	利得
losses	损失
journal	日记账
bank saving	银行存款
deposit	存款
merchandise	商品
intangible	无形资产
fixed assets	固定资产
short-term loans	短期借款
long-term loans	长期借款
tax payable	应交税费
wages and salaries payable	应付工资和薪金
the cost of goods sold	主营业务成本
other receivable	其他应收款
surplus reserve	盈余公积
double-entry bookkeeping	复式记账
trial balance	试算平衡表

Exercises

I. Answer the following questions.

1. How do we distinguish accrual basis accounting from cash basis accounting?
2. How many elements does accounting include?
3. What is the fundamental accounting equation?

II. Choose the best answer for each of the following statements.

1. Which of the following should be recorded on cash-basis? _____.
   A. Purchases of inventory on account   B. Sales on account
   C. Paying off loans   D. All of the above
2. The economic resources of a business are called_____.
   A. assets   B. liabilities   C. owner's equity   D. receivables
3. The purchase of office suppliers on account will_____.
   A. increase an asset and increase a liability
   B. increase an asset and increase an owner's equity
   C. increase one asset and decrease another asset
   D. increase an asset and decrease a liability
4. Which of the following accounts is a liability account? _____.
   A. Prepaid rent   B. Advertising
   C. Unearned expenses   D. Withdrawals
5. Please select the item which does not belong to the current liabilities. _____.
   A. Accounts payable   B. Payables to employees
   C. Interest payable   D. Long-term payables
6. Which of the following items is an expense? _____.
   A. Accounts payable   B. Cost of goods sold
   C. Accounts receivable   D. Prime operating revenue
7. Which of the following accounts does not belong to the category of the asset accounts? _____.
   A. Cash   B. Wages payable   C. Notes payable   D. Prepaid insurance
8. A business has assets of $140,000 and liabilities of $60,000. How much is its owner's equity? _____
   A. $ 0   B. $140,000   C. $ 80,000   D. $ 200,000

III. Decide whether each statement is true or false.

1. In cash basis accounting, cash receipts are treated as revenues and cash payments are handled as expenses.   (   )

2. GAAP required that businesses use the cash basis accounting.   (   )

3. In accrual-basis accounting, the accounting records a transaction only when cash is received or paid.   (   )

4. Revenue is earned when the business has delivered a completed goods or service to the customer.   (   )

5. Increase in expenses will decrease assets and increase owners' equity.   (   )

6. All receivables are liabilities, while all payables are assets.   (   )

7. Assets are the resources of value that are owned and will result in future economic outflow to an entity.   (   )

8. Liability represents the entity's future economic obligations, which also reflects the creditors' claims on the company's assets.   (   )

IV. Translate the following sentences into Chinese.

1. The net income is the difference between the cash receipts (revenues) and the cash payments (expenses).

2. The accrual-basis accounting is designed to avoid misleading income statement results that could result from the timing of cash receipts and payments.

3. Liability is a future sacrifice of economic benefits arising from present obligations of an entity as a result of the past transactions or events.

4. Owner's equity increases with revenue, and decreases because of expenses or an owner's withdrawal.

5. The accounting equation should remain in balance at all times because of double–entry accounting or bookkeeping. (Double-entry means that every transaction will affect two accounts in the general ledger.)

Reading Materials

Cost Accounting and Cost Management

Cost accounting provides information for management accounting and financial accounting. Cost accounting measures, analyzes, and reports financial and non-financial information relating to the costs of acquiring or using resources in an organization.

For example, calculating the cost of a product is a cost accounting function that answers financial accounting's inventory valuation needs and management accounting's decision-making needs. Modern cost accounting takes the perspective that collecting cost information is a function of the management decisions being made.

Thus, the distinction between management accounting and cost accounting is not so clear-cut, and we often use these terms interchangeably in the book.

We frequently hear business people use the term cost management. Unfortunately, that term has no uniform definition.

We use cost management to describe the approaches and activities of managers in short run and long run planning and control decisions that increase value for customers and lower the costs of products and services.

For example, managers make decisions regarding the amounts and kinds of materials being used, changes in plant processes, and changes in product designs, information from accounting systems helps managers to manage costs, but the information and the accounting systems themselves are not cost management.

Cost management has a broad focus and should not be interpreted to mean only continuous reduction in costs. Planning and control of costs are usually inextricably linked with revenue and profit planning. As part of cost management managers often deliberately incur additional costs, for example in advertising and product modifications, to enhance revenues and profits.

Cost management is not practiced in isolation. It's an integral part of general management strategies and their implementation. Examples include programs that enhance customer satisfaction and quality, as well as research and development and marketing programs.

Chapter 3   Double-Entry Bookkeeping

After studying this chapter, you should be able to:

- List types of commonly used accounts;
- Comprehend debit and credit principle;
- Understand nature and function of double-entry bookkeeping;
- Explain basic rules for double-entry bookkeeping.

Before we study double-entry bookkeeping, we should understand the general information about the account and grasp the debit-credit bookkeeping.

3.1   Accounts

At first, we should understand the meaning of the account. Accounts are used to maintain an orderly record of any economic transaction or process data systematically, reflecting the change of the accounting elements (i.e. decrease or increase). An account is made up of two basic parts, as is shown in Figure 3-1. If the left side represents the increase, the right side records the decrease accordingly, which forms the basic structure of an account. A T-account is always used by accountants to record transaction. The account title rests on the horizontal line at the top of T, and vertical line divides the account into left and right sides, which we refer to as debit and credit.

Debit	the Name of the Account	Credit
Beginning balance		
Increases	Decreases	
Ending balance		

Figure 3-1   Structure of Accounts

The numerous accounts in the account book are called ledger accounts. There are two types of ledgers in ordinary use: general ledgers and subsidiary (or specific) ledgers. An account usually shows four kinds of amounts in a specific accounting period, namely the beginning balance, increase sum, decrease sum and ending balance. The relationship among them is shown below:

Ending Balance = Beginning Balance + Increase Sum − Decrease Sum

3.1.1　Account Titles

Account titles are used to name the accounting elements that are classified scientifically. It is the name of an account. It requires a trial balance at the end of a certain accounting period to check whether the records in the general ledger are correct. Therefore, account titles' design lay the foundation of keeping an account.

In China, there are six groups of account titles such as assets, liabilities, common subjects, owners' equity, costs, profits and losses. The chart of accounts is uniform and applied in accounting. The chart of accounts, sometimes called the code of accounts, is a listing of the accounts by title and numerical designation.

3.1.2　Types of Commonly Used Accounts

The specific accounts used by a company depend on the nature of the company's business. Each company must design its accounts in a way that will reflect the nature of its business and the needs of its management in directing the business. There are, however, accounts that are common to most business. Remember that the total balances of the asset accounts equal to the balances of the liability accounts plus the balances of the owner's equity accounts.

Assets　A company must keep records of the increases and decreases in each asset that it owns. Some of the most common asset accounts are as follows.

Cash　It is the title of the account used to record increases and decreases in cash. Cash consists of money or any medium of exchange that a bank will accept at face value for deposit. Included are coins, currency, check, postal and express money order, certificates of deposit, and money deposited in a bank or banks.

Notes receivable　A promissory note is a written promise to pay a definite sum of money at a fixed future date. Amounts due from others in the form of promissory notes are recorded in an account called notes receivable.

Accounts receivable　Companies often sell goods and services to customers on the basis of oral or implied promises to pay in the future, such as in thirty days or at the first of the month. These sales are called credit sales, or sales on account, and the promises to pay are known as accounts receivable.

Land and Buildings　Increases and decreases in land and buildings owned by a business are recorded in accounts called land and buildings, respectively. The reason is that the building is subject to wear and tear, but the land is not.

Equipment　A company may own many different types of equipment. Usually there is a separate account for each type of equipment.

Liabilities　It is debt. It is important to keep records of what the company owes as it is to keep asset accounts. There are two types of liabilities: short term and long term. The following accounts are short-term liabilities.

Notes payable   The account called notes payable is the exact opposite of notes receivable. It is used to record increases and decreases in promissory notes owed to creditors.

Accounts payable   It is the opposite of accounts receivable. It represents amounts owed to creditors on the basis of an oral or implied promise to pay. Accounts payable usually arise as the result of the purchase of merchandise, services, supplies, or equipment on credit.

Owner's equity   The claim that the owner has on the assets of the business is called owner's equity. Owner's equity is often split into separate accounts for the owner's capital balance and the owner's withdrawals.

Capital   This account shows the owner's claim to the assets of the business. After total liabilities are subtracted from total assets, the remainder is the owner's capital. The balance of the capital account equals the owner's investments in the business plus its net income and minus net losses and the owner's withdrawals.

Withdrawals   When the owner withdraws cash or other assets from the business for personal use, its assets and its owner's equity both decrease. To separate these two amounts for decision-making, businesses use a separate account for withdrawals. This account shows a decrease in owner's equity.

Revenues   The increase in owner's equity from delivering goods or services to customers or clients is called revenue. The ledger contains as many revenue accounts as needed, such as lawyer's service revenue account, businesses' interest account and rent revenue account.

Expenses   The cost of operating a business is called expense. Expenses have the opposite effect of revenues, so they decrease owner's equity. A business needs a separate account of its expenses, such as salary expense, rent expense, advertising expense, and utilities expense. Expense accounts are decreases in owner's equity.

3.2   Debit and Credit Principle

The methods used to record economic transaction are single-entry system and double-entry system. The latter is considered as the heart of modern accounting, and now it is widely used all over the world. Based on the accounting equation, double-entry accounting means each transaction is recorded in at least two accounts with equal amounts. In double-entry accounting, when debit and credit used as the symbol of account entries, the method called debit-credit bookkeeping.

The T-account is the basic form of the double-entry system and debit-credit bookkeeping, with the debit on the left and the credit on the right. Debit-credit bookkeeping obeys the following basic rules:

(1) Using the "debit" and "credit" as the sign for recording transaction in accounts;

(2) Basing on the principle of "debits accompanied with credits in equal amounts".

By convention, increases in asset and expenses are entered as debits while increases in liability, capital and income are recorded as credits. Decreases in asset and expense are recorded as credits, while decreases in liability, capital and income, are entered as debits. Table 3-1 summarizes the rules.

Table 3-1   Principles of Debit-credit Bookkeeping

Debit (on the left side)	Account	Credit (on the right side)
increase	Asset	decrease
increase	Costs	decrease
increase	Expense	decrease
decrease	Liabilities	increase
decrease	Owners' equity	increase
decrease	Revenue	increase

3.3   Double-Entry Bookkeeping

3.3.1   The Nature and Function of Double-Entry Bookkeeping

In accountancy, double-entry bookkeeping system is the basis of the standard system used by businesses and other organizations to record financial transactions. It was first described by Italian mathematician Luca Pacioli. Its premise is that a business's financial condition and results of operations are best recorded in accounts. Each account maintains a "history" of changes in monetary values about a particular aspect of the business.

3.3.2   Basic Rules for Double-Entry Bookkeeping

Double-entry bookkeeping is based on the accounting equation and debit-credit principle and uses certain signs of accounting to present increases and decreases of special accounting items. It is a system that records two aspects of every transaction. Every transaction is both a debit in one account and a corresponding credit in another. The transaction should be recorded in two accounts at least with equal amounts.

Every transaction will result in the changes of several items, at least two items, that is to say every transaction should be illuminated twice simultaneously in debit and credit. So we can obtain the same value in debit and credit. Each transaction has two effects and it is referred to as dual aspect or the duality convention. It is a technique of recording transactions as they occur so that summaries may be made of the transactions and presented as a report to the users of accounts.

The double-entry principle works on the basis of an equation of assets and liabilities. For any purchase of goods on credit, under the double-entry system, entries are made in the account to reflect both of the receipts of goods and also the creation of liabilities to the business. After the entries are recorded, the goods will be recorded as the assets of business while the creditor, to whom money is owed by the business for the supply of goods, remains as a liability of the business.

The basic rules for double-entry bookkeeping are very important. The direction for accounting elements is as shown in Figure 3-2.

Name of the Account	
the increase of the asset	the decrease of the asset
the decreases of the liabilities	the increases of the liabilities
the decrease of the capital	the increase of the capital
the transfer of the sales	the happening of the sales
the happening of the expenses	the transfer of the expenses

Figure 3-2　The Direction for Accounting Elements

【Example 3.1】

Cash		Capital	
Dr.			Cr.
July 1, investor 5,000			July, 1 cash 5,000

3.4　The Bookkeeping for Assets, Liabilities and Capital

【Example 3.2】

B Company had the following assets and liabilities on 1 February.

Land	Building	Inventories	Receivables	Cash	Bank	Payables	Loan
200	60	10	15	5	32	17	240

Basing on the accounting equation we can defer that: Capital=Assets−Liabilities= 322−257=65

1. Enter the opening balances into the ledger account (b/d);

2. Analyze the transaction by using the double-entry bookkeeping.

(1) Bought the building whose value is 20, paying 15 by cheque, the balance to be paid at the end of the month;

(2) Bought inventories costing 25, paying 15 by cheque, the balance to be paid at the end of the month;

(3) Returned some inventory to his supplier because they existed faulty; whose value was 10;

(4) Received 8 from his receivables. They all paid him by cheque.

The posting of the beginning balance is as follows:

The changes:

Building: b/d 60, debit 20(1)

Bank: b/d 32, credit 15(1), credit 15(2), debit 8(4)

Payables: b/d 17, credit 5(1), credit 10(2), debit 10(3)

Inventories: b/d10, debit 25(2), credit 10(3)

Receivables: b/d15, credit 8(4)

The Account of Building

	Debit	Credit	Balance
THE B/D			60
HAPPENING	20		80

The Account of Bank

	Debit	Credit	Balance
THE B/D			32
HAPPENING		15	
HAPPENING		15	
HAPPENING	8		10

The Account of Payables

	Debit	Credit	Balance
THE B/D			17
HAPPENING		5	
HAPPENING		10	
HAPPENING	10		22

The Account of Inventories

	Debit	Credit	Balance
THE B/D			10
HAPPENING	25		
HAPPENING		10	25

The Account of Receivables

	Debit	Credit	Balance
THE B/D			15
HAPPENING		8	
BALANCE			7

The changes of debit: 63   the changes of credit: 63

Happening: the debit = the credit

3.5   The Bookkeeping for Expenses and Revenues

1. The account

Revenue: the cost of goods sold, inventory, purchase

Inventory: only recording beginning and ending, without the purchase

Purchase: only recording the purchase of inventory

2. Transactions

In the month of May, we assume the company occurred some transactions as follows:

March 1, BR starts business as a sole proprietor with $20,000 in cash;

March 2, pays $15,000 cash into a business bank account;

March 4, purchases goods on credit from JM for $2,000;

March 6, purchases goods from ERD on credit for $3,000;

March 7, pays wages in cash for $60;

March 10, pays rent by cheque for $80;

March 12, sells goods in cash for $210;

March 16, buys furniture for $1,500 paying by cheque;

March 19, sells goods on credit to SP for $580;

March 22, buys goods in cash for $3,900;

March 24, buys fittings in cash for $600;

March 25, pays wages in cash for $110;

March 26, sells goods in cash for $430;

March 27, receives part payment from SP of $330 by cheque;

March 28, pays advertising by cheque for $25; sells goods in cash for $890;

March 29, sells goods on credit to KM for $8,090;

March 30, withdraws $100 cash for his personal use.

3. Accounting records

Accounting records are as follows:

(1)	Debit. Cash	20,000	
	Credit. Capital		20,000
(2)	Debit. Bank	15,000	
	Credit. Cash		15,000
(3)	Debit. Purchases	2,000	
	Credit. Payables-JM		2,000
(4)	Debit. Purchases	3,000	
	Credit. Payables-ERD		3,000
(5)	Debit. Wages	60	
	Credit. Cash		60
(6)	Debit. Rent	80	
	Credit. Bank		80
(7)	Debit. Cash	210	
	Credit. Revenues		210
(8)	Debit. Furniture	1,500	
	Credit. Bank		1,500
(9)	Debit. Receivables-SP	580	
	Credit. Revenues		580
(10)	Debit. Purchases	3,900	
	Credit. Cash		3,900
(11)	Debit. Fittings	600	
	Credit. Cash		600

Key Words and Phrases

account	会计账户
debit	借方
credit	贷方
beginning balance	期初余额
ending balance	期末余额
ledger	分类账
general ledgers	总分类账
subsidiary/specific ledgers	辅助/明细分类账
single-entry system	单式记账法
double-entry system	复式记账法
account title	会计科目
trial balance	试算平衡
chart of accounts	科目表

asset	资产
wear and tear	自然损耗
capital	资本
withdrawal	抽资，退股
credit side	贷方
creditor	债权人
debit side	借方
currency	现金
face value	面值
account payable	应付账款
account receivable	应收账款
liability	负债
owners' equity	所有者权益
note receivable	应收票据
net earning	净收益
on account	赊账

Exercises

I. Answer the following questions.

1. What are the three basic types of accounting? Name two additional types of accounts.

2. Interpret the debit-credit principle.

3. What is the double-entry bookkeeping?

II. Choose the best answer for each of the following statements.

1. An account has two sides called_____.

 A. debit and credit   B. asset and liability

 C. revenue and expense   D. journal and ledger

2. Which of the following accounting titles belongs to an asset account? _____

 A. Selling expenses   B. Prepayments by customers

 C. Account receivable   D. All of the above

3. The left side of an account is referred to as _____.

 A . the balance B. a footing C. a credit D. a debit

4. The purchase of land for cash is recorded by a _____.

 A. debit to Cash and a credit to Land B. debit to Cash and a debit to Land

 C. debit to Land and a credit to Cash D. credit to Cash and a credit to Land

5. The account credited for a receipt of cash on account is _____.

 A. cash   B. service revenue

C. accounts payable   D. accounts receivable

6. When a company gets a loan, which accounts are both increased with the same amount? _____.

    A. Assets and liabilities   B. Assets and owner's equity

    C. Liabilities and owner's equity   D. Assets and income

7. Please select the item which doesn't belong to the current liabilities? _____.

    A. Accounts payable   B. Payables to employees

    C. Interest payable   D. Long-term payables

8. In accounting practice, which item can't be accounted into the manufacturing cost? _____.

    A. Direct material   B. Manufacturing overhead

    C. Administrative expense   D. Direct labor

III. Decide whether each statement is true or false.

1. By convention, asset and expenses increases are entered as credits while liability, capital and income increases are recorded as debits.   (   )

2. In the accounting entry, fixed assets are always debited, and cash in bank or notes payable is credited.   (   )

3. Debit-credit bookkeeping obeys the basic rules that accounts contain at least one account debited and at least one account credited.   (   )

4. A client pays $1,000 to a company for goods, then the company debits cash.   (   )

5. In China, there are three groups of account titles.   (   )

6. Increases and decreases in land and buildings owned by a business are recorded in the same accounts.   (   )

7. The withdrawal account shows a decrease in owner's equity.   (   )

8. The double entry principle works on the basis of an equation of assets and liabilities and debit-credit principle.   (   )

IV. Translate the following sentences into Chinese.

1. Accounts are used to maintain an orderly record of any economic transaction or process data systematically, reflecting the change of the accounting elements (ie. decrease or increase).

2. It requires a trial balance at the end of a certain accounting period to check whether the records in the general ledger are correct.

3. Based on the accounting equation, double-entry accounting means each transaction is recorded in at least two accounts with equal amounts.

4. The chart of accounts, sometimes called the code of accounts, is a listing of the accounts by title and numerical designation.

5. The balance of the capital account equals the owner's investments in the business plus its net income and minus net losses and the owner's withdrawals.

Reading Materials

Management and Administration of a Company

A director is a person who acts as the director in essence no matter what the person is called; and the person is entitled to join in the board of directors and perform voting right. In common the status of director is determined by meeting of shareholders; and the company acts stipulate some restricts regarding the appointment of director supervisor or senior executive of a company.

None of the following persons may hold the position of director, supervisor or senior executive of a company:

- A person without capacity or with restricted capacity for civil acts;
- A person who was sentenced to criminal punishment for the crime of embezzlement, bribery, seizure of property or misappropriation of property or for undermining the socialist market economy order, where not more than five years have elapsed since the expiration of the enforcement period; or a person who was deprived of his political rights for committing a crime, where not more than five years have elapsed since the expiration of the enforcement period;
- A director, or factory head or manager of a bankrupt and liquidated company or enterprise who was personally responsible for the bankruptcy of the company or enterprise, where not more than three years have elapsed since the date of completion of the bankruptcy liquidation;
- A legal representative of the company or enterprise that had the business license revoked for violating the law, where such legal representative bears individual liability therefore and not more than three years have elapsed since the date of revocation of the business license;

When a company elects or appoints a director or supervisor or engages senior executives in violation of the preceding paragraph, such election, appointment or engagement shall be invalid. Where any director, supervisor or senior executive of a company during his term of office occur any circumstance as listed above, the company shall remove him from office.

Quiz 1

1. Avalon gives his customers individual trade discounts from the list price and a general 5% cash discount for all invoices settled within 7 days of issue. A new customer, Nolava negotiates a 25% trade discount. His transactions during June are:

June 12, buys goods with a £5,000 list price;

June 15, returns goods with a £1,000 list price as faulty;

June 16, pays half of the net balance on his account.

How much does Nolava owe Avalon at the end of June? (　　).

    A. £1,425　　　　　B. £1,500　　　　　C. £2,000　　　　　D. £2,850

2. Jasmine buys goods from Reshma on 60-day credit terms. Alternatively, a 10% cash discount is available on any payment received within 10 days. During February the following transactions took place:

Feb 2, Jasmine buys £800 of goods;

Feb 11, Jasmine pays Reshma a cheque for £360.

What is the balance of Jasmine's account in Reshma's sales ledger on 28 February? (　　).

    A. £360　　　　　B. £400　　　　　C. £440　　　　　D. £485

3. What document is usually sent every month from the supplier to the customer, listing all the transactions between them during that month? (　　).

    A. Invoice　　　B. Receipt　　　C. Statement　　　D. Credit note

4. Manish buys goods on credit from Lisa but finds that some of them are faulty. What document would Manish return to Lisa with the faulty goods? (　　).

    A. Statement　　　B. Debit note　　　C. Sales invoice　　　D. Purchase invoice

5. What business document provides proof of payment for a business transaction? (　　).

    A. Invoice　　　B. Receipt　　　C. Claim　　　D. Debit note

6. What is the purpose of crossing a cheque? (　　).

    A. To stop it being paid into an account other than the payee's

    B. To speed up the time it takes to go through the clearing system

    C. To allow it to be paid into any account, not just the payee's

    D. To tell the bank to check that there is enough money in the account to pay it

7. Christa pays her mortgage by instructing her bank to make monthly payments of a fixed amount from her current account, when the mortgage rate changes her issues revised instructions to the bank. Which method of payment is Christa using? (　　).

    A. Standing Order　　B. Payable Order　　C. Direct Debit　　D. Crossed Cheque

8. Alfredo is the Managing Director of a large engineering company. He signs his name on a company cheque for £260 in accordance with the bank mandate. The company name appears on the cheque. If the bank dishonors the cheque as the company has insufficient funds in the account, who is liable for the £260? (　　).

    A. The engineering company　　　　　B. Alfredo

    C. The bank　　　　　D. No one

9. Which of the following items would be likely to be paid out of petty cash? (　　).

    (i) payment to window cleaner £10;

    (ii) hire purchase payment for a delivery van £123;

    (iii) a payment for postage stamps £11.60;

    (iv) a payment to a supplier for goods bought on credit of £65.

    A. All of the above　　B. i, iii and iv　　C. i only　　D. i and iii

10. Boris is employed as an accounting technician in the purchase ledger section of a contract cleaning company. Upon making a payment to a supplier, what is the sequence of events that Boris should carry out? (   ).

    A. Draw up a cheque for signing, check invoice with goods received note, check invoice with purchase order, check invoice calculation

    B. Check invoice with purchase order, draw up a cheque for signing, check invoice with goods received note, check invoice calculation

    C. Check invoice with purchase order, check invoice with goods received note, check invoice calculation, draw up a cheque for signing

    D. Check invoice calculation, draw up a cheque for signing, check invoice with purchase order, check invoice with goods received note

11. Which of the following represents the correct imprest amount in an imprest petty cash system? (   ).

    A. Notes and coins in the cash box – vouchers – IOUs

    B. Notes and coins in the cash box + vouchers – IOUs

    C. Notes and coins in the cash box – vouchers + IOUs

    D. Notes and coins in the cash box + vouchers + IOUs

12. Louise introduces her car into her business. Which parts of the business' accounting equation will change? (   ).

    A. Assets and capital   B. Capital and profit

    C. Liabilities and assets   D. Capital and liabilities

13. Which of the following should be classified as current liabilities? (   ).

    (i) Trade debtors

    (ii) VAT payable

    (iii) Trade creditors

    (iv) Drawings

    A. i and ii   B. ii and iii   C. iii and iv   D. ii and iv

14. Which item will appear as a debit balance in the ledger accounts? (   ).

    A. Capital   B. Bank overdraft   C. Creditors   D. Stock

15. Which of the following balance sheet summaries is correct? (   ).

Capital   Assets   Liabilities

    A. £35,000 £24,000 £11,000   B. £21,000 £15,000 £36,000

    C. £25,000 £33,000 £8,000   D. £33,000 £25,000 £8,000

16. Joanne has just started-up a business. She introduced £10,000 of her own savings, equipment worth £2,500 and obtained a bank loan of £1,000.

What is the correct balance on Joanne's capital account following these transactions? (   ).

    A. £10,000   B. £13,500   C. £12,500   D. £11,000

17. Which of the following is the correct posting to record a cash purchase of £300 from Amdale? (   ).

A. Debit Purchases £300　Credit Amdale £300

B. Debit Amdale £300　Credit Purchases £300

C. Debit Purchases £300　Credit Bank £300

D. Debit Bank £300　Credit Purchases £300

18. Which of the following items would appear on opposite sides of a trial balance? (　　).

　　A. Stock and Drawings　　　　　B. Sales and Returns out

　　C. Carriage in and Carriage out　　D. Debtors and Returns out

19. East buys goods from South on credit. Which one of the following is the correct double entry for this transaction in East's books? (　　).

　　A. Dr. Purchases, Cr. Cash　　　　B. Dr. Purchases, Cr. South

　　C. Dr. Cash, Cr. Purchases　　　　D. Dr. South, Cr. Purchases

20. The following entry appeared in a cash account in March, payments by debtors £15,000, rent received £250, insurance paid £150, drawings £700, capital paid in £2,000. The balance on 1st March was 2,000, what was the closing balance on 31st March? (　　).

　　A. £ 14,400　　　B. £18,400　　　C. £15,800　　　D. £10,400

21. The following entries appeared in the purchase ledger control account for February. Balance b/f 1st February £1,700, purchases £18,000, paid to suppliers £10,000, discount received £1,200, purchases returns 3,000. What was the balance on 28th February? (　　).

　　A. £ 5,500　　　B. £2,100　　　C. £11,500　　　D. £7,900

22. Which of the following would normally be classified as a selling overhead? (　　).

　　A. Advertising　　　　　　　　B. Delivery van expenses

　　C. Insurance premiums paid　　　D. Telephone expenses

23. Janice buys a dress costing £120, shoes costing £60 and a jacket costing £190. These are all gross figures, inclusive of VAT at 17.5%. How much VAT in total has Janice paid? (　　).

　　A. £55.11　　　B. £64.75　　　C. £74.48　　　D. £68.51

24. Sarah runs her own business and is registered for VAT. This week her purchases were £2,350 *inclusive* of VAT and her sales were £1,000 *exclusive* of VAT. The rate of VAT is 17.5%. At the end of the week what will the VAT account in her ledger show? (　　).

　　A. £350 debtor　　B. £350 creditor　　C. £175 debtor　　D. £175 creditor

25. Indris is a VAT registered trader. On 1 October he purchases carpets for his new showroom at the list price of £2,000. He is given a trade discount of 20% and the VAT rate is 17.5%. What sum will Indris be invoiced, inclusive of VAT? (　　).

　　A. £1,980　　　B. £2,350　　　C. £1,600　　　D. £1,880

26. Which of the following is a record of prime entry? (　　).

　　A. Debtors ledger control account　　B. Journal

　　C. Purchase invoice　　　　　　　D. Trial balance

27. Which one of the following is the correct posting from the purchase day book? (　　).

　　A. Dr. General ledger purchase account, Cr. Suppliers' accounts in purchase ledger

B. Dr. General ledger purchase account, Cr. Cash book

C. Dr. Suppliers' accounts in purchase ledger, Cr. General ledger purchase account

D. Dr. Cash book, Cr. General ledger purchase account

28. Jonathan sends a debit note to one of his suppliers. In which of Jonathan's books of prime entry would this be recorded? (　　).

　　A. Sales　　　　　　B. Purchases　　　C. Sales returns　　D. Purchase returns

29. In which books of prime entry would the following transactions be entered? (　　).

　　A credit sale for £387 and a cash sale of £200 less 10% discount for cash payment.

　　A. The cash book and sales day book

　　B. The petty cash book and sales day book

　　C. The purchase day book and sales day book

　　D. The journal and cash book

30. Rivano has a balance of £350,000 on his purchase ledger control account at the end of May. What does this mean? (　　).

　　A. He has bought £350,000 of goods in May

　　B. He is owed £350,000 by his customers

　　C. He owes £350,000 to his suppliers

　　D. He has paid £350,000 to his suppliers in May

31. Which of the following is an example of an item of revenue expenditure? (　　).

　　A. Insurance of goods in transit to customers

　　B. Import duties charged on a new fixed asset for the business

　　C. Wages of employees installing a new fixed asset for the business

　　D. A new delivery van

32. Which of the following is an example of an item of capital expenditure? (　　).

　　A. Capital introduced　　　　　　　　B. Purchase of fixed assets by bank

　　C. Purchase of inventory　　　　　　　D. Telephone expenses paid by bank

33. Which of the following would *normally* be entered through the journal? (　　).

　　A. Credit purchase returns　　　　　　B. Transfers between accounts

　　C. Receipts from credit customers　　　D. Expense payments

34. Which journal entry correctly records the credit purchase of plant and equipment? (　　).

　　A. Dr. the supplier's personal account, Cr. Plant and Equipment

　　B. Dr. Cash, Cr. Plant and Equipment

　　C. Dr. Plant and Equipment, Cr. the supplier's personal account

　　D. Dr. Plant and Equipment, Cr. Cash

35. Seb packs goods on an assembly line. He is paid a different amount each week, depending on his output of assembled goods.

　　By what method of remuneration is Seb paid? (　　).

A. Piecework   B. Commission   C. Hourly paid   D. Salaried

36. For the month of May, the following figures have been extracted from a trader's records concerning wages.

(i) Employees' NI £678

(ii) Gross basic wages £9,900

(iii) PAYE £2,000

(iv) Employer's NI £925

What will be the total charge for wages and salaries in the final accounts? (   ).

A. £10,825   B. £10,578   C. £11,503   D. £13,503

37. Anish manufactures wooden pallets and employs people on a piece rate scheme of £2.00 per pallet made. If an employee produces more than 200 pallets in a week, any extra pallets made over 200 are paid at a rate of £3.00 per pallet. All employees have a guaranteed minimum weekly wage of £375. Last week an employee produced 235 pallets. What will the employee's gross pay be for last week? (   ).

A. £400   B. £375   C. £505   D. £370

38. Which of the following would be classed as revenue expenditure for a shop? (   ).

(i) Assistants' wages

(ii) Business rates paid

(iii) Purchase of a new shop counter

(iv) Repainting the outside of the shop

A. i and ii   B. i, ii and iii   C. i, ii and iv   D. iii and iv

39. An item of capital expenditure was incorrectly treated as revenue expenditure. What effect did this have on the accounts? (   ).

A. Expenses were understated and fixed assets understated

B. Expenses were overstated and fixed assets understated

C. Expenses were understated and fixed assets overstated

D. Expenses were overstated and fixed assets overstated

40. Output VAT is _____?

A. VAT charged on goods and services sold by a business

B. VAT charged on goods and services sold by a VAT registered trader

C. VAT paid on goods and services bought in by a business

D. VAT payable on the profits earned on a particular sale

41. The total of the discounts allowed column in the cash book is £150. How should this item be posted in the ledger? (   ).

A. Dr. Discount Allowed   B. Cr. Discount Allowed

C. Dr. Discount Received   D. Cr. Discount Received

42. Which of the following is not an example of a fixed asset? (   ).

A. Plant and machinery   B. Building

C. Motor vehicle   D. Goodwill

43. Which of the following is the correct posting to record a discount received from a supplier? (   ).

    A. Dr. Creditors, Cr. Bank

    B. Dr. Debtors, Cr. Bank

    C. Dr. Creditors, Cr. Discounts received

    D. Dr. Debtors, Cr. Discounts received

44. Which of the following will help to reduce overdue balances in sales ledger accounts? (   ).

    A. Improved debt collection methods

    B. An increase in the bank overdraft facility

    C. Trade debtors paying invoices more slowly

    D. An increase in credit facilities to customers

45. Which of the following is not an example of a fixed asset? (   ).

    A. Plant and machinery

    B. Building

    C. An investment in the shares of another company

    D. Goodwill

46. Which of the following methods of payment is Tariq most likely to use to pay for his weekly food shopping? (   ).

    A. Debit card   B. Standing order   C. Direct debit   D. Bankers draft

47. Selina receives a cheque from her sister. What term describes Selina's role in this transaction? (   ).

    A. Payer   B. Drawer   C. Payee   D. Drawee

48. Goods received note is used by a business to _____?

    A. order goods from a supplier

    B. record the receipt of goods from a supplier and to input information to the business accounting system

    C. notify the supplier that goods have been received safely

    D. instruct the accounts department to pay the invoice for the goods

49. The owner of a small business draws out some money for personal use. Which of the following correctly states the effect of the drawings upon the accounting equation? (   ).

    A. Assets increase, capital increases   B. Assets decrease, capital increases

    C. Assets decrease, capital decreases   D. Assets decrease, liabilities decrease

50. Which is the correct double entry for the write-off of a bad debt? (   ).

    A. Dr. Debtors, Cr. Bad debts   B. Dr. Creditors, Cr. Bad debts

    C. Dr. Bad debts, Cr. Debtors   D. Dr. Bad debts, Cr. Creditors

Chapter 4 Journalizing and Posting Transaction

After studying this chapter, you should be able to:

- Understand definition and types of journals;
- Illustrate what elements are included in the general journal entry;
- Explain the special journal;
- Learn how to deal with posting transaction.

4.1 Journals

The analysis of each transaction is kept in a financial record called a journal. This is the first step that accountants record transaction in the book. The record is really diary of business activities that lists events involving financial affairs—transactions—as they occur. That is, a journal is a chronological (day–by–day) record of all business transactions, and each transaction is registered in the order of date.

The accountants record the transactions in the journals include:

(1) Identify the transaction from source documents, such as bank deposit slips, sales receipts, and cheque stubs.

(2) Specify each account affected by the transaction and classify it by type (asset, liability, or owner's equity).

(3) Determine whether each account is increased or decreased by the transaction.

(4) Use the rules of debit and credit to determine whether to debit or credit the account.

(5) Enter the transaction in the journal, including a brief explanation for journal entry. Accountants write the debit side of the entry first and the credit side next.

According to their different contents, journals may be grouped into general journals and special journals.

4.1.1 General Journal

A general journal can be used to record all types of transactions that a business has. All transactions include at least two accounts. When more than two accounts are affected, it is called a compound journal entry. A business may use a single all-purpose two-column journal, or it may use a number of multicolumn journals.

To illustrate how transactions are entered in this journal, let us consider again the financial affairs of the Pick'n Pay Holding Ltd.

When the owner, Raymond Ackerman, invested $80,000 to start the firm, the accountant analyzed the transaction and identified the following effects.

a. The business had $80,000 of property in the form of cash.

b. Ackerman had an $80,000 financial investment in the business.

Then, using this analysis as a guide, the accountant knew that transaction should be entered as follows.

a. Debit and Cash account to record the increase in the asset cash.

b. Credit the R. Ackerman, Capital accounts to record the new ownership interest.

The accountant's written record of the analysis of the transaction appears in the general journal shown in Table 4-1.

Table 4-1

GENERAL JOURNAL   Page 1

DATE	DESCRIPTION OF ENTRY	POST REF.	DEBIT		CREDIT	
			80,000	00	80,000	00
20X7	Cash					
Sep.1	R. Ackerman, Capital					
	Beginning investment of owner					

Note that the journal entry includes (a) the date of the transaction, (b) the title of the account debited (placed flush left) and the title of the account credited (indented slightly), (c) the dollar amounts of the debit (left) and the credit (right)—dollar signs are omitted in the money columns— and (d) a short explanation of the transaction.

First, each page in the general is given a number and that the year is recorded at the top of the date column. The month and day are also written in the date column on the first line of the first entry. After the first entry, the year and the month are recorded only when a new page is begun or when either the year or the month changes. However, the day of each transaction is written in the date column on the first line of each entry.

The account to be debited is always recorded first in the description of entry column. The account title is written close to the left margin, and the credit amount is then entered on the same line in the debit column. The account to be credited is always recorded on the line beneath the debit. The account title is indented about half an inch from the left margin. And the credit amount is entered on the same line in the credit column.

A brief explanation follows the credit part of the entry. This explanation begins at the left margin of the description of entry column so that as much space as possible is available.

Explanation should be complete and concise. Whenever possible, the explanation for a journal entry should include a description of the source of the information contained in the entry. For example, if a check is written to make a payment, the explanation in the journal entry for that transaction should include the check number. Similarly, if goods are purchased on credit, the explanation in the journal entry should show the number of the supplier's invoice. These source document numbers are part of an audit trail—a chain of references that makes it possible to trace information about transaction through the accounting process.

Account titles are written in the general journal exactly as they appear in the chart of accounts and in the accounts themselves. The exact wording of each account title minimizes the possibility of errors when the figures are transferred to the account. The transfer of information from the general journal to the accounts is the next step in the accounting process.

Accountants usually leave a blank line between each general journal entry. This separates the transactions and makes them easier to identify and read. Some accountants prefer to use this blank line to number each general journal entry for identification purposes. Because the accountant writes the transaction analysis in a journal before making any entry in the accounts, a journal is sometimes referred to as a record of original entry. The process of recording data in a journal is called journalizing. By journalizing first, the accountant knows that all the information about a transaction is recorded in one place before any details can be forgotten.

4.1.2　Special Journal

A special journal is a journal that is used to record only one type of transaction. The way to save writing and posting labor is to divide the transactions into groups according to their type and to record them respectively in special journal. For example, the sales journal is used to record only sales of merchandise on credit. Generally, merchandising businesses use the following journals in their accounting system in Table 4-2.

Table　4-2

Type of Journal	Purpose
JOURNALS	
Sales Journal	To record sales of merchandise on credit.
Purchases Journal	To record purchases of merchandise on credit.
Cash Receipts Journal	To record the cash received from all sources, including cash sales and cash collected on account from credit customers.
Cash Payments Journal	To record all cash paid out.
General Journal	To record any transaction that does not belong to a special journal, and to record the adjusting and closing entries.

The special journal also can be entered by some specific business with the same nature including cash on hand journals, cash in bank journals and transfer account journals. In China, cash on hand journal and cash in bank journal are widely used than others. Cash on hand journal is applied in a company to conduct accounting and supervision on the cash on hand concerning daily receipt, disbursement and balance. There are some main columns for the date, document's type and number, digest, opposite account, debit, credit and balance, etc. For the document's type, we can fill in with "cash receipt", "cash payment", "bank deposit receipt" or "bank deposit payment". Cash in bank journal is the journal used for daily cash in bank, and it is entered almost in the same way as cash on hand journal. Refer to Table 4-3 and Table 4-4.

Table 4-3   Cash on Hand Journal

Year		Document		Digest	Opposite Account	Debit	Credit	Balance
Month	Date	Type	No.					
Dec.	1st			Opening balance				4,000
Dec.	3rd	Payment	1	Withdrawal for use	Cash in bank	600		4,600
Dec.	5th	Payment	2	Expense for water and electricity	Administrative expenses		3,000	1,600
Dec.	12th	Payment	15	Payment for wages	Wages payable		600	1,000
Total								1,000

Table 4-4   Cash in Bank Journal

Year		Document		Digest	Opposite Account	Debit	Credit	Balance
Month	Date	Type	No.					
Dec.	1st			Opening balance				5,000
Dec.	3rd	Payment	1	Withdrawal for use	Cash on hand		600	4,400
Dec.	5th	Receipt	3	Receipt from accounts receivable	Accounts receivable	3,000		7,400
Dec.	12th	Payment	15	Payment for wages	Wages payable		1,200	6,200
Total								6,200

4.2 Posting Transaction

Posting is the process of copying journal entry information from the journal to the ledger. Before we prepare the financial statement, we must prepare the trial balance. And before we prepare the trial balance, we must determine the balance of each specific account by posting. To do this, we should post the entries listed in the journal into their respective ledger accounts. The debits and credits in the journal will be accumulated into the appropriate debit and credit columns of each ledger page.

Ledgers include two types of ledgers: general ledger and subsidiary ledger. The general ledger is the book used to list all the accounts established by an organization. The chart of accounts, also called the code of accounts, is established to achieve it. The chart of accounts is a listing of titles and numbers of all accounts found in the general ledger. It serves both an index to the ledger and a description of the accounting system and also serves a link between financial statements and the ledger. The account titles should be grouped by or in the order of the five major sections of the general ledger (asset, liabilities, owners' equity, revenues, expenses). The number of accounts may be two or more digits, according to the size of the company. In China, the chart of accounts is regulated by the accounting system of MOF and all companies use the unified chart of accounts. The chart of accounts in China is four-digit system. Subsidiary ledger is set up in accordance with the specific accounts and classified to record the economic activities with more detailed information. A company will only have one general ledger, but it can have multiple subsidiary ledgers. The balance of the general ledger is equal to the sum of balances in its subsidiary ledgers.

The posting of journal entry to ledger is performed in the following steps:

1. Record the date and the amount of the entry in the account.

2. Insert the number of the journal page in the PR column of the account.

3. Insert the ledger account number in the PR column of the journal.

In the month of May, we assume the company occurred some transactions as follows:

March 1, BR starts business as a sole proprietor with $20,000 in cash;

March 2, pays $15,000 cash into a business bank account;

March 4, purchases goods on credit from JM for $2,000;

March 6, purchases goods from ERD on credit for $3,000;

March 7, pays wages in cash for $60;

March 10, pays rent by cheque for $80;

March 12, sells goods in cash for $210;

March 16, buys furniture for $1,500 paying by cheque;

March 19, sells goods on credit to SP for $580;

March 22, buys goods in cash for $3,900;

March 24, buys fittings in cash for $600;

March 25, pays wages in cash for $110;

March 26, sells goods in cash for $430;

March 27, receives part payment from SP of $330 by cheque;

March 28, pays advertising by cheque for $25; sells goods in cash for $890;

March 29, sells goods on credit to KM for $8,090;

March 30, withdraws $100 cash for his personal use.

4. Accounting records are as follows:

(1) Debit. Cash   20,000

     Credit. Capital   20,000

(2) Debit. Bank   15,000
        Credit. Cash   15,000
(3) Debit. Purchases   2,000
        Credit. Payables-JM   2,000
(4) Debit. Purchases   3,000
        Credit. Payables-ERD   3,000
(5) Debit. Wages   60
        Credit. Cash   60
(6) Debit. Rent   80
        Credit. Bank   80
(7) Debit. Cash   210
        Credit. Revenues   210
(8) Debit. Furniture   1,500
        Credit. Bank   1,500
(9) Debit. Receivables-SP   580
        Credit. Revenues   580
(10) Debit. Purchases   3,900
        Credit. Cash   3,900
(11) Debit. Fittings   600
        Credit. Cash   600

Posting to the Ledger

	Debit	Credit
CAPITAL		20,000
CASH	20,000+210+430+890	15,000+60+3,900+600+110+100
BANK	15,000+330	80+1500+25
PURCHASES	2,000+3,000+3,900	
PAYABLES-JM		2,000
PAYABLES-ERD		3,000
WAGES	60+110	
RENT	80	
ADVERTISING	25	
SALES		210+580+430+890+8,090
FURNITURE	1,500	
FITTING	600	
RECE-SP	580	330
RECE-KM	8,090	
DRAWING	100	

Key Words and Phrases

journals	日记账
post	过账
chronological record	序时账簿
general journal	普通日记账
special journal	特殊日记账
journal entry	日记账分录
compound journal entry	复合分录
two-column journal	两栏式日记账
multicolumn journals	多栏式日记账
account title	会计名称
cash on hand journal	现金日记账
cash in bank journal	银行存款日记账
transfer account journal	转账日记账
receipt	收入
disbursement	支出
balance	余额
date column	日期栏
document's type and number column	凭证的类型和编号栏
digest column	摘要栏
opposite account column	对应科目栏
debit column	借方栏
credit column	贷方栏
balance column	余额栏
cash receipt	现收
cash payment	现付
bank deposit receipt	银收
bank deposit payment	银付
opening balance	期初余额
withdrawal for use	提现备用
receipt from accounts receivable	收到应收账款
cash on hand	库存现金

Exercises

I. Answer the following questions.

1. What are the five steps when the accountants record the transactions in the journals?
2. Explain the journal entry. What content does it include?
3. What is the posting? Interpret its four steps.

II. Choose the best answer for each of the following statements.

1. Why do accountants record transactions in the journal? _____.
   A. To ensure that all transactions are posted to the ledger.
   B. To ensure that total debits equal total credits
   C. To have a chronological record of all transaction
   D. To help prepare the financial statements

2. Posting is the process of transferring information from the _____
   A. journal to the trial balance   B. ledger to the trial balance
   C. ledger to the financial statements   D. journal to the ledger

3. Sales on account should be recorded in_____.
   A . sales journal   B. purchases journal
   C. cash receipts journal   D. cash payments journal

4. The records that are kept for the individual asset, liability, equity, revenue, expenses, and dividend components are known as _____.
   A. accounts   B. ledgers   C. journals   D. trial balance

5. _____ is a listing of titles and numbers of all accounts found in the general ledger.
   A. General ledger   B. Subsidiary ledger
   C. Chart of accounts   D. Financial statements

6. In China, the uniform chart of accounts regulated by MOF is_____.
   A. two digits   B. three digits   C. four digits   D. more than four digits

7. Which of the following is a liability account?_____.
   A. Prepaid Insurance   B. Additional Paid-In Capital
   C. Salaries Payable   D. Accumulated Depreciation

8. Which of the following is a contra asset account?_____.
   A. Inventory   B. Equipment
   C. Accumulated Depreciation   D. Retained Earnings

III. Decide whether each statement is true or false.

1. The general journal can be used to record only one type of transaction.   (   )
2. A business may use a single all-purpose two-column journal, or it may use a number of

multicolumn journals. ( )

3. It is not necessary that the explanation for a journal entry should include a description of the source of the information contained in the entry. ( )

4. Bank statement is the record document which reflects the company's bank savings and usage in its bank of deposit. ( )

5. Posting is the process of copying journal entry information from the ledger to the journal. ( )

6. A company will only have one general ledger, but it can have multiple subsidiary ledgers. ( )

7. The subsidiary ledger is a single ledger. ( )

8. Controlling accounts are accounts in the general ledger. ( )

IV. Translate the following sentences into Chinese.

1. A journal is a chronological (day–by–day) record of all business transactions, and each transaction is registered in the order of date.

2. The exact wording of each account title minimizes the possibility of errors when the figures are transferred to the account.

3. The special journal also can be entered some specific business with the same nature including cash on hand journals, cash in bank journals and transfer account journal.

4. The debits and credits in the journal will be accumulated into the appropriate debit and credit columns of each ledger page.

5. Subsidiary ledger is set up in accordance with the specific accounts and classified to record the economic activities with more detailed information.

Reading Materials

Accounting Information Systems

1. The features of an effective accounting information system. An effective accounting information system should capture and summarize transactions quickly, accurately, and usefully. It should generate a variety of accounting reports, including financial statements and trial balances, that aid management in operation a business. The four major aspects of a good accourtting system are (1) control over operations, (2) compatibility with the particular features of business, (3)flexibility in response to changes in the business, and (4) a favorable cost/benefit relationship such that bentfits outweigh costs.

2. How computerized and manual accounting systems are used, computerized accounting system process inputs faster than do manual systems and can generate more types of reports. The key components of a computerized accounting system are hardware, software, and company personnal. Account numbers play a bigger role in the operation of computerized systems than they

do in manual systems, because computers classify accounts by account numbers. Both computerized and manual accounting systems require transactions to be classified by type. Computerized systems use a menu structure to organize accounting functions. Posting, trial balances, financial statements, and closing procedures are carried out automatically in a Computerized accounting system. Computerized accounting system are integrated so that the different modules of the system are updated together.

3. Use the sales journal, the cash receipts journal, and the accounts receivable subsidiary ledger, manual accounting system use special journal to record transactions by category. Credit sales are recorded in a sales journal, and cash receipts in a cash receipts journal.

Quiz 2

1. A business buys machinery costing 2000 yuan and sells machinery for 1800 yuan in the year. The opening balance of the equipment account is 2000 yuan. What will be the balance brought down in the next period? (   ).

    A. Dr. 1,800   B. Dr. 2,200   C. Cr. 1,800   D. Cr. 2,200

2. A business buys equipment costing 1000yuan and sells equipment for 800yuan in the year. The opening balance of the equipment account is 1000yuan. What will be the balance carried down to the next period? (   ).

    A. Dr. 800   B. Dr. 1,200   C. Cr. 800   D. Cr. 1,200

3. A business has a bank overdraft of ￥350 and ￥50 cash in hand at the end of the accounting period. What balances will be brought down at the start of the next accounting period? (   ).

    A. Dr. Bank   B. Cr. Cash   C. Dr. Cash   D. Cr. Bank

4. A capital account has a credit balance of ￥40000. What balances will occur at the end of the year to take this balance into the next period? (   ).

    A. Dr. capital balance c/d   Cr. capital balance b/d

    B. Dr. capital balance c/d   Dr. capital balance b/d

    C. Cr. capital balance c/d   Dr. capital balance b/d

    D. Cr. capital balance c/d   Cr. capital balance b/d

5. Which of the following is a current asset? (   ).

    A. Bank deposit account   B. Premises

    C. Computer   D. Tools

6. Which of the following is not an item of capital expenditure? (   ).

    A. Capital

    B. Purchase of a new motor van

    C. Purchase of a second hand factory machine

    D. Replacement of his managing director's car

7. Which of the following types of expenditure would generally be classified as revenue

expenditure? (   ).

    A. Payment of tax

    B. Purchase of a delivery van by a courier service

    C. Extension to the office building of a toy manufacturer

    D. Swivel chairs for resale by an office equipment retailer

8. Which of the following types of expenditure would be classified as capital expenditure? (   ).

    A. Installation for the fixed assets   B. Rent of a building

    C. Capital introduced   D. Telephone

9. Which of the following types of expenditure would be classified as capital expenditure? (   ).

    A. Legal fees associated with the purchase of an office

    B. Repairs to an equipment

    C. Rent of a long lease hold property

    D. Capital introduced

10. Which of the following is not a book of prime entry? (   ).

    A. Petty cash book   B. Cash book   C. Journal   D. Sales ledger

11. What is the purchases ledger? (   ).

    A. A record of the credit limits of each credit supplier

    B. A record of the personal details of each credit supplier

    C. A record of the accounts of each credit supplier

    D. A record of the accounts of each credit customer

12. What is the general ledger? (   ).

    A. The book where all transactions are originally recorded before being posted to ledger accounts

    B. The book which contains a ledger account for each type of asset, liability, expense and income

    C. The book which contains all of the details of the fixed assets

    D. The book which contains all of the details of the trade debtors

13. When an expense is paid in cash, _____.

    A. net assets increase and profit increases

    B. net assets decrease and profit decreases

    C. net assets remain the same and profit increases

    D. net assets remain the same and profit decreases

14. What of the following would be a debit balance on the ledger account? (   ).

    i sales   ii purchase   iii expense   iv capital

    A. i and ii   B. i and iii   C. i and iv   D. ii and iii

15. What is a book of prime entry? (   ).

    A. A ledger account where transactions are originally recorded

B. A record in which transactions are originally recorded before being transferred to a ledger account

C. A separate ledger where details of a particular type of transaction are recorded in parallel to the recording in the general ledger

D. A set of memorandum ledger accounts which back up the total figures recorded in the general ledger

16. Which of the following is a current liability? (   ).

    A. Trade debtors   B. Trade creditors   C. Bank   D. Capital

17. Which of the following is a current liability? (   ).

    A. Trade debtors   B. Bank overdraft   C. Cash   D. Inventory

18. Which of the following is current asset? (   ).

    A. Inventory   B. Bank overdraft   C. Creditors   D. Fixed asset

19. Which of the following is current asset? (   ).

    A. Owners' equity   B. Petty cash

    C. Sales man's motor car   D. Computer soft wares

20. Which of the following describes the accounting equation? (   ).

    A. net assets = capital – profit – drawings

    B. net assets = capital – profit + drawings

    C. net assets = capital + profit + drawings

    D. net assets = capital + profit – drawings

21. When stock is purchased on credit, _____.

    A. net assets and owners' capital do not change

    B. net assets increase and owners' capital increases

    C. net assets decrease and owners' capital decreases

    D. net assets increase and owners' capital stays the same

22. Which of the following describes the separate entity principle? (   ).

    A. The fixed assets of a business are a separate entity from the current assets

    B. The drawings of a business are a separate entity from the profit of the business

    C. The business is a separate entity from the owner of the business

    D. The owner of the business must be a separate entity from a lender to the business

23. Which of the following is an example of consideration in a contract? (   ).

    A. Accepting an offer   B. Being old enough to enter into legal relations

    C. Making an offer   D. Paying for the goods

24. Which of the following is the best remedy for a breach of a contract where the supplier has delivered goods and the purchaser has refused to pay? (   ).

    A. Action for price   B. Damages   C. Repudiation   D. Specific performance

25. Which of the following is source document? (   ).

    A. Paying in slip   B. Statement   C. Delivery note   D. Goods received note

Chapter 5　Trial Balance and Adjustment

After studying this chapter, you should be able to:

- Understand the content and classification of the trial balance;
- Illustrate procedures for preparing a trial balance;
- Identify the errors and treat errors;
- Learn how to adjust transactions.

5.1　Introduction to Trial Balance

After all transactions for the period have been posted to the ledger accounts, the balance for each account is determined. Every account has either a debit, credit, or zero balance. Since equal dollar amount of debits and credits are entered in the accounts for every transaction recorded, the sum of all the debits in the ledger must be equal to the sum of all the credits. In order to make sure the total debits of all ledger accounts are equal to total credits of them, we should prepare a trial balance. While editing accounting treatment, we often make errors, how to scan the errors? The most direct method is also to make an initial trial balance.

5.1.1　The Content of the Trial Balance

It is a summary listing of both the balances and the titles of accounts. A trial balance not only provides a check on the equality of debits and credits but is also a useful summary of account balances for preparing financial statement. A list of accounts which is classified into debit and credit should have equal amount. After posting, we can obtain the trial balance. This doesn't prove there are no errors. On the contrary if the totals of the debit and credit balances entered on the trial balance are not equal, then there must be errors. If the trial balance does not balance, it indicates that we can not go further into preparation of the financial statements. An error exists somewhere and must be detected and corrected before proceeding.

At the end of an accounting period, you will prepare three trial balance:

(1) An unadjusted trial balance is prepared for using your general ledger account balances before you make adjusting entries.

(2) An adjusted trial balance is done after preparing adjusting entries and posting them to your general ledger. This will help ensure that the books used to prepare your financial statements are in balance.

(3) A post-closing trial balance is done after preparing and posting your closing entries. This trial balance, which should contain only sheet accounts, will help guarantee that your books are in balance for the beginning of the new accounting period.

5.1.2   The Classification of the Trial Balance

Total amounts for all the accounts happening on debit = total amounts for all the accounts happening on credit

The total balance of all the accounts on debit = the total balance of all the accounts on credit

Supplementary: Probable errors in journalizing are as follows.

Reversal entry, omission error, duplication error, commission error, principle error.

5.1.3   The Balance of the Account

Assets and expenses:

Beginning balance in the assets + increases on debit side − decreases on credit side = ending balance

Liabilities, equity, income:

Beginning balance in the account + increases on credit side − decreases on the debit side = ending balance

The total of credit side = the total of debit side

5.1.4   The Functions of a Trial Balance

(1) It is the starting point at preparing financial statement such as income statement and balance sheet.

(2) It shows the current balances on all the asset, liability, capital, income, expenses. This can help provide useful information to management.

(3) It is a method to check errors in accounting system and we can correct them.

5.1.5   Procedures for Preparing a Trial Balance

(1) Listing the account titles in the trial balance.

(2) Recording balances of each account, entering debit balances in the left column and credit balances in the right column.

(3) Totaling the debit and credit columns.

(4) Comparing the totals.

Assets and expenses accounts are debited for increases and would normally have debit balances. Liabilities, owners' equity, and income accounts are credited for increases and would normally have credit balances. If the totals of debits and credits agree, the trial balance is in balance.

5.2　Identification of Errors

There are two types of errors: one which does not affect the trial balance and the other which does.

If the totals of the debit and credit balances entered on the trial balance are not equal, then an error or errors must have been made.

If the total of all the accounts on credit side ≠ the total of all the accounts on debit side, there must be errors.

5.2.1　The Classifications of Errors

(1)　In the posting of the transactions to the ledger accounts;

(2)　In the balancing of the accounts;

(3)　In the transferring of the balances from the ledger accounts to the trial balance.

5.2.2　Other Errors

There are still some errors that do not destroy the equivalence of the trial balance.

(1)　Errors of omission, duplication of entries, errors of principle, errors of commission, errors of original entry, reversal of entry, compensating errors;

(2)　Errors of commission：the selection of account is wrong, but the two accounts are the same in nature which will not affect the balance sheet and income statement;

(3)　Errors of principle: the selection of account is wrong; they have different nature which will influence the income statement and balance sheet.

【Example 5.1】

(1)　The paying of 100 yuan for office commodity is debited to purchases account instead of to the office expenses, the error is known as an error of principle errors.

(2)　The purchasing of inventory on credit should be credited into the payables—A company, but wrongly credited to payables—B company, and the debit is correct. The error is known as commission errors.

5.3　The Treatment of Errors

5.3.1　Errors in the Account Balances or Preparing the Trial Balance

The errors can't be corrected through editing account treatment. What we could do is to correct them immediately on the trail balance.

5.3.2 Errors Recognized by the Trial Balance

(1) Transactions are recorded incorrectly, with different amounts on the debit side and the credit side of the ledger account.

(2) Transaction is recorded twice as a debit entry or twice as a credit entry, instead of being recorded as a debit in one account and a credit in another.

For such errors, the total of the debit columns in the trial balance will not be the same as the total of the credit columns.

For instance, if only one error is made in our cash books, 208 dollars was received on 1 May, year 2008 from Company KK, the entry should book like this:

Cash Book

Year 8			Dollars			
May 1	Company KK		208			

Sales Ledger—Company KK

			Year 8		Dollars
			May 1	Cash	28

In our books, we have put 208 dollars on the debit side, and also 28 dollars on the credit side. When we draw up a trial balance statement, its totals will be different by 180 dollars.

5.3.3 Errors Unidentified by the Trial Balance

These errors will lead to and result in the same amount of debits being entered as there were credits or no entry being made either on the debit or credit side. The implication is that if the trial balance would have balanced before the error. It would also show a balance figure after the error. This includes as follows:

Errors of omission, duplication of entries, errors of principle, errors of commission, errors of original entry, reversal of entry, compensating errors, transposition errors.

5.4 Suspense Accounts

When the trial balance does not balance, every effort should be made to find the errors and correct them, but occasionally they cannot be found quickly and in these circumstances a suspense account is opened and used to record the difference until the errors can be found.

The use of the suspense account allows financial statements to be prepared subject to the correction of the errors. The prudent approach is to treat the suspense account balance as an expense (rather than an asset) if it is a debit balance and as a liability (rather than as revenue) if it is a credit balance. When the errors are found they should be corrected and an explanation given.

If the error relates to the debit side and credit side, at the same time, the corrections are made through the journal in the first instance, and then in the ledger accounts.

If the error is one that has affected the agreement of the trial balance, then the suspense account will be involved in the correction of the error.

In fact, it refers to the errors in one side. We should present the true entry in the appropriate side and on the other hand represent the suspense account at the same time on the contrary side.

5.5 Adjustments for Transactions

5.5.1 Principle for Adjustments

First we should base on the accounting equation.

Equation 1: **Assets = Liabilities + Owners' Equity**

Equation 2: **Profit = Revenues − Expenses**

Equation 3: **Assets = Liabilities + Owners' Equity + (Revenues - Expenses)**

Then we should understand the relationship of debits and credits of accounts.

The total amount of debts for all the accounts = the total amount of credits for all the accounts.

5.5.2 The Procedure

(1) Identify the category for every item in the given trial balance.

How to identify the category? We can classify it into 3 groups which should be shown in the balance and which are stated in the income statement, and which is an item of trade account?

Account of Assets

the beginning balance of the assets

decreases

increases

the ending balance of the assets

Account of Equity

decreases

the ending balance of equity

increases

the ending balance of equity

Accounts of Expenses

increases | decreases

Accounts of Revenues

decreases | increases

(2) Pay attention to the extra events in accounting.

(Identify which items it may influence)

- Accruals and prepayments;
- Bad debts and allowance for receivables;
- Depreciation;
- Errors which should be corrected (omitted generally).

5.5.3 Preparation of the Income Statement and Balance Sheet

Obtain the net profit of the income statement and post to the balance sheet.

Obtain the total number of the debits and credits, finding out if the balance is equal.

Preparation of the income statement and balance sheet can also include the following.

- Giving the trial balance before the adjustment;
- Giving the balance sheet and income statement;
- Analyzing the characteristic of the extra event;
- Showing the Income Statement and Blance Sheet in the working paper as changes;
- Showing the final financial statement after adjustment.

【Example 5.2】

1. Trial balance of company A on 30 December, 2007

ITEMS	DEBIT	CREDIT
Sales		125,658
Returns	6,341	1,902
Receivables and payables	11,257	7,983
Equipment	10,000	
accumulated depreciation		1,550
Purchases	44,726	
Beginning inventory	5,000	
Carriage inwards	908	
Carriage outwards	272	
Wages and salaries	11,550	
Rent and local taxes	8,800	
Office expenses	2,681	
Bank deposit	10,000	
Bank	4,797	
Discount allowed and received	5,652	3,765
Sales tax payable		1,325
Beginning capital		4,300
Drawing	14,799	
Loan		10,300
Tobal	156,783	156,783

Notes:

A. The amount of returns from debits and credits

(a) The returns at debit 6341 relates to the revenue which is the contra account of revenue and it should subtract from the revenue.

(b) The returns at credit 1902 relates to the purchase which is the contra account of purchase and it should subtract from it.

B. Discount allowed and received

(a) Discount allowed relates to the expense and it should list on the income statement as an expense which should be deducted from the revenue.

(b) Discount received related to the revenue and it should list on the income statement as revenue which should be added to the revenue.

C. How to obtain the cost of goods sold using the materials about inventory?

The cost of goods sold = Beginning inventory + Purchase + Carriage inwards – Returns –

Ending inventory

When completing the accounting we can obtain the key item in the income statement which should be deducted from the revenue.

2. Giving the financial statement.

(1) The balance sheet

BALANCE SHEET

Asset		Liabilities	
Non-current asset		Non-current asset	
Equipment		Loan	
Depreciation		Current liabilities	
Net balance		Account payables	
Current asset		Current asset	
Bank deposit		Interest payables	
Bank		Sales tax payables	
Receivables		Sub total	
Bad debt		Owners' equity	
Net balance		Beginning capital	
Accrued interest receivables		Add: net profit	
Inventory		Drawing	
		Capital balance	
		Sub total	
TOTAL		TOTAL	

(2) The income statement

	Original	Changes	Ending balance
Sales Revenue			
– Returns			
– Cost of goods sold			
Beginning inventory			
+ Purchases			
+ Carriage inwards			
– Returns			
– Ending inventory			
– Gross profit			
+ Bank deposit interest			
+ Discount received			
– Bank charge			

续表

	Original	Changes	Ending balance
– Carriage outwards			
– Wages and salaries			
– Rent and local taxes			
– Discount allowed			
– Bad debts			
– Depreciation			
= Net profit			

(3) Labeling the trial balance and posting them into the balance sheet.

BALANCE SHEET

Asset		Labilities	
Non-current asset		Non-current liabilities	
Equipment	10,000	Loan	10,300
Depreciation	1,550	Current liabilities	
Net balance	8,450	Account payables	7,983
Current Asset		Interest payables	
Bank deposit	10,000	Sales tax payables	1,325
Bank	4,797	Sub total	
Receivables	11,257	Owenr's equity	
Bad debt		Beginning capital	4,300
Net balance		Add: net profit	
Accrued interest receivables		Drawing	14,799
Inventory	5,700	Capital balance	
		Sub total	
TOTAL		TOTAL	

(4) Labeling the trial balance and posting them into the income statement.

Income Statement

		Original	Changes	Ending balance
Sales				125,658
– Returns				6,341
– Cost of goods sold				63,032

续表

Income Statement	Original	Changes	Ending balance
Beginning inventory			5,000
+ Purchases			64,726
+ Carriage inwards			908
– Returns			1,902
– Ending inventory			5,700
= Gross profit			56,285
+ Bank deposit interest			
+ Discount received			3,765
– Bank charges			
– Carriage outwards			272
– Wages and salaries			11,550
– Rent and local taxes			8,800
– Discount allowed			5,652
– Bad debts			
– Depreciation			
Office expense			2,681
= Net profit			31,095

5.5.4   Analyzing the Characteristic of the Extra Event

【Example 5.3】

(1) The bank deposit was made on June 30. This account earns interest at 10% per annual. The balance shown in the ledgers is the only principle and the interest should be accounted and post to the ledger.

Analysis:

Interests: 10000×8%÷2=400

Interest revenue increases 400   Accruals receivable increases 400

Income statement item (credit)   Balance statement item (debit)

(2) Bank charges accrued to 30 December 2007 are estimated to be 100Yuan.

Analysis:

Expenses: increases 100   Accruals payable increases 100

Income statement item (debit)   Balance statement item (credit)

(3) Office equipment is to be depreciated at 1% every month.

Analysis:

Depreciation expenses 10000×0.01=100   Accumulated depreciation 100

Income statement item (debit)   Balance statement item (credit) >the contra of equipment

(4) Following a review of receivables at the year-end, it is decided that a bad debt of 1207 should take place, and an allowance for receivables made of 2%.

(5) The ending inventory on hand on 30 December 2007 was 5700 Yuan.

Analysis:

★ A bad debt of 1,207 should happen, which results the deceases of the receivables 1,207.

Expenses: 1,207 (debit)   Receivables: 1,207 (credit)

★ The bad expenses increase (11,257−1,207)×0.02 = 201, account receivables decrease 201

Expenses: 201 (debit)   Receivables: 201 (credit)

5.5.5 Showing Them in the Working Paper as Changes

- Dr. Interest receivables   400   Dr. Interest expenses 100
-    Cr. Interest revenue   400   Cr. Interest payables100
- Dr. ad expenses 100   Dr. Bad debts expenses 1408
-    Cr. ad   100   Cr. Account receivables1408

Balance Sheet				Liabilities and Owner's equity		
Equipment	10,000		10,000	Loan	10,300		10,300
Depreciation	1,550	100	1,650	Current liabilities			
Net balance	8,450		8,350	Account payables	7,983		7,983
Current asset				Interest payables			
Bank deposit	10,000		10,000	Sales tax payables	1,325		1,325
Bank	4,797		4,797	Sub total			
Receivables	11,257		11,257	Owners' equity			
Bad debt		1,408	1,408	Beginning capital	4,300		4,300
Net balance			9,849	Add: net profit			
Accrued interest receivables		400	400	Drawing	14,799		14,799
Inventory	5,700		5,700	Capital balance			
				Sub total			
TOTAL			39,096	TOTAL			

Adjusted Income Statement

Income statement			
	Original	Changes	Ending balance
Sales			125,658
− Returns			6,341
− Cost of goods sold			63,032
Beginning inventory			5,000
+ Purchases			64,726

续表

Income statement

	Original	Changes	Ending balance
+ Carriage inwards			908
− Returns			1,902
− Ending inventory			5,700
= Gross profit			56,285
+ Bank deposit interest		400	400
+ Discount received			3,765
− Bank charges		100	100
− Carriage outwards			272
− Wages and salaries			11,550
− Rent and local taxes			8,800
− Discount allowed			5,652
− Bad debts		1,408	1,408
− Depreciation		100	100
Office expenses			2,681
= Net profit			29,887

Adjusted Balance Sheet

Asset		Changes	Balances	Liabilities		Changes	Balances
Non - current asset				Non - current liabilities			
Equipment	10,000		10,000	Loan	10,300		10,300
Depreciation	1,550	100	1,650	Current liabilities			
Net balance	8,450		8,450	Account payables	7,983		7,983
Current asset				Interest payables			100
Bank deposit	10,000		10,000	Sales tax payable	1,325		1,325
Bank	4,797		4,797	Sub total			
Receivables	11,257		11,257	Owners' equity			
Bad debt		1,480	1,480	Beginning capital	4,300		4,300
Net balance				Add: net profit	29,887		29,887
Accused interest receivables		400	400	Drawing	14,799		14,799
Inventory	5,700		5,700	Sub total			
Total				Total			39,096

Key Words and Phrases

ledger account	分类账
trial balance	试算表
adjustment	账项调整
adjusted trial balance	账项调整后的试算表
accounting treatment	会计处理
financial statements	财务报表
sheet accounts	资产负债表账户
income statement	损益表
general ledger	总分类账
reversal entry	颠倒入账错误
omission error	省略错误
duplication error	复制错误
commission error	代理错误
principle error	原则性错误
accruals and prepayments	收益和提前还款
bad debts	坏账
depreciation	折旧，贬值
net balance	净余额
accrued interest receivable	应收利息
carriage inward	运入运费
ending inventory	期末存货
gross profit	毛利
discount received	购货折扣
discount allowed	销货折扣
bank deposit	银行存款
sales tax payable	应付销售税
beginning capital	期初资本
capital balance	资本项目差额

Exercises

I. Answer the following questions.

1. What is a trial balance?
2. Describe the basic steps of preparing the trial balance.

3. Explain the uses of the trial balance.

II. Choose the best answer for each of the following statements.

1. Trial balance can be used_____.

   A. to show the financial position of a business.

   B. to show the operation of a business.

   C. to show the cash flow of a business.

   D. as a tool that is used to alert you to errors in your books.

2. Which of the following will have an impact on the balance of the trial balance? _____.

   A. Forgetting to record a journal entry as a general ledger transaction.

   B. Neglecting to make a journal entry at all.

   C. The purchase of equipment was incorrectly charged to expense.

   D. Errors in addition of trial balance.

3. Which of the following are correct? _____.

   A. If the trial balance is in balance, we can say that all transactions have been correctly analyzed and recorded in the proper accounts.

   B. If a transaction was completely omitted and not be recorded in the journal, the trial balance is still in balance.

   C. The trial balance provides a general check on the accuracy of recording and posting.

   D. An adjusted trial balance is done after preparing and posting your choosing entries.

4. If the debit and credit totals of the trial balance do not agree, the probable reasons include_____.

   A. the entering of a debit as a credit or vice versa.

   B. clerical errors in copying account balances into the trial balance.

   C. listing a debit balance in the credit column of the trial balance, or vice versa.

   D. enter equal amount in credit and debit but the amount is wrong.

5. Trial balance is the part of_____.

   A. balance sheet   B. the statement of owner's equity

   C. the income statement   D. none of the above

6. The trial balance is _____.

   A. internal records   B. outsider reports

   C. both internal records and outsider reports   D. none of the above

7. The accountants prepare the trial balance after_____.

   A. making the journal   B. posting to ledger

   C. preparing the financial reports   D. occurring of the transaction

III. Decide whether each statement is true or false.

1. If the trial balance is in balance, we can say that all transactions have been correctly

analyzed. (   )

2. If the debit and credit totals of the trial balance do not agree, it indicates that we must make some mistakes. (   )

3. The trial balance lists all account titles in the subsidiary ledger. (   )

4. If we record a transaction in an incorrect account, the trial balance will not be in balance. (   )

IV. Translate the following sentences into Chinese.

1. In order to make sure the total debits of all ledger accounts is equal to total credits of them, we should prepare a trial balance.

2. An unadjusted trial balance is prepared for using your general ledger account balances before you make adjusting entries.

3. An adjusted trial balance is done after preparing adjusting entries and posting them to your general ledger.

4. A post-closing trial balance is done after preparing and posting your closing entries.

5. Liabilities, owners' equity, and income accounts are credited for increases and would normally have credit balances.

Reading Materials

The trial balance is a list of the account titles in the ledger with their respective debit and credit balances. It can be used to prove whether the total of the debits in the ledger is equal to the total of the credits, and can also be as a tool to detect errors. Whilst the trial balance is a good method to check arithmetic accuracy and the double-entry rule, there are some errors which the balance will not disclose to you. They are as follows:

(1) Entries made to the wrong side of each account;

(2) Transactions omitted or entered twice;

(3) Incorrect amounts entered on both sides;

(4) Entries made in the wrong accounts, though correct sides (allocation error);

(5) Compensating errors that cancel one another out.

To locate trial balance errors, the following is a guide:

(1) Re-add columns to confirm error;

(2) Check each ledger account has its correct balance individually;

(3) Ensure each ledger account balance is correctly listed upon the trial balance.

(4) Subtract the total debit from the total credit and ensure the following difference:

a. The difference indicates an omitted posting;

b. Half the difference indicates a posting to the wrong side;

c. A difference divisible by 9 indicates a transposition figure (e.g. 649 instead of 946).

(5) Check the balance in each ledger account by re-adding debit and credit columns and checking the subtraction to determine the account balance;

(6) Check all the posting back to the journal and source documents.

Quiz 3

1. A sole trader has net assets of 19,000yuan on 30 April 2003. During the year to 30 April 2000, he introduced 9800yuan additional capital into the business. Profits were 8000yuan, of which he withdrew 4200yuan. His capital on 1 May 2002 was (   ).

    A. 3,000   B. 5,400   C. 13,000   D. 16,600

2. A company achieves a gross profit of 20% on sales. Opening inventory was 5,000yuan, payables at the start of the period were 4,000 yuan. Sales in the period amounted to 50,000yuan. Year end payables were 6,000yuan and the business had paid payables 37,000yuan. All the inventory had been stolen at the end of the period, what was its value? (   ).

    A. 0   B. 2,000   C. 6,500   D. 4,000

3. A business achieves a margin of 25% on sales. Opening inventory was 18,000yuan, closing inventory was 28,000yuan and purchases totaled 300,000yuan. Calculate the sales for the period. (   ).

    A. 386,666   B. 362,500   C. 413,230   D. 400,000

4. If sales were 25,500, and cost of sales was 21,250, what was the gross profit percentage? (   ).

    A. 16.67%   B. 20%   C. 83.333%   D. 120%

5. The bookkeeper has disappeared. There is no cash in the till and theft is suspected. It is known that the cash balance at the beginning of the year was 240yuan. Since then, total sales have amounted to 41,250yuan. Credit customers owed 2,100yuan at the beginning of the year and owe 875yuan now. Cheques banked from credit customers have totaled 24,290yuan. Expenses paid from the till receipts amount to 1,850yuan and cash receipts of 9,300yuan have been lodged in the bank.

How much has the bookkeeper stolen during the period? (   ).

    A. 7,275   B. 9,125   C. 12,155   D. 16,575

6. A business has opening inventory 15,000yuan, achieves a mark-up of 25% on sales, sales totaled 50,000yuan, purchases were 420,000yuan. Calculate closing inventory. (   ).

    A. 15,000   B. 20,000   C. 60,000   D. 35,000

7. A business sells goods earning a constant 25% mark up. Sales in period amounted to 500,000yuan. Opening inventory was 10,000yuan, closing inventory is valued at 20,000yuan. Purchases were 450,000yuan. The owner suspects theft; calculate the amount of the inventory losses. (   ).

    A. 40,000   B. 65,000   C. 60,000   D. 50,000

8. A business commenced with a bank balance of 3,250 yuan. It subsequently purchased goods on credit for 1,000 yuan, gross profit mark-up was 120%; half the goods were sold for cash, less cash discount of 5%; all takings were banked.

The resulting net profit was (   ).

    A. 700   B. 3,700   C. 5,450   D. 5,700

9. An organization's cash book has an opening balance in the bank column of 485yuan credit. The following transactions then took place.

Cash sales 1,450yuan including VAT of 150yuan.

Receipts from customers of debts of 2,400yuan.

Payments to payables of debts of 1,800yuan less 5% cash discount.

Dishonored cheques from customers amounting to 250yuan.

The resulting balance in the bank column of the cash book should be (   ).

    A. 1,255 debit   B. 1,405 debit   C. 1,905 credit   D. 2,375 credit

10. During the year, all sales were made at a gross profit margin of 15%. Sales were 25500yuan, purchases were 22,000yuan and closing inventory was 4,000yuan. What was the opening inventory? (   ).

    A. 3,675   B. 4,000   C. 4,174   D. 4,325

11. During the year all sales were made with a 20% mark-up on cost. Sales were 25,500yuan, purchases were 26,000yuan and closing inventory was 10,000yuan. What was opening inventory? (   ).

    A. 4,150   B. 5,250   C. 10,000   D. 14,750

12. At 1/1/x1/ receivables owed 3,050yuan, at 31/12/x1 they owed 4,000yuan, cash received from receivables during the year was 22,000yuan(including 1,000 bad debt recovered). All sales were made at a 20% gross profit margin and no inventory are held.

What were purchases for the year? (   ).

    A. 21,950   B. 18,292   C. 17,560   D. 4,390

13. If the mark-up is 30% and the cost of the sales is 28,000yuan, and expenses are 14000yuan, what is the net profit? (   ).

    A. Profit 2,000yuan   B. Loss 2,000yuan

    C. Profit 5,600yuan   D. Loss 5,600yuan

14. A sole trader has net assets of 19,000yuan on 30 April 20x0. During the year to 30 April 20x0, he introduced 9,800yuan additional capital into the business. Profits were 8,000yuan, of which he withdrew 4,200yuan. His capital at 1 May 20x9 was(   ).

    A. 3,000   B. 5,400   C. 13,000   D. 16,600

(PS: In this quiz, the currency unit it yuan.)

Chapter 6　Financial Statement

After studying this chapter, you should be able to:

- Understand the financial statements;
- Understand the principle for editing balance sheet;
- Understand the principle for editing income statement;
- Grasp the format to edit the cash flow statement;
- Identify the relationship between balance sheet and income statement.

6.1　Balance Sheet

After the journalizing and posting of adjusting entries, adjusted trial balance can be worked out. The financial statements are prepared by using the account balances founded on the adjusted trial balance.

Financial reports are the final products of accounting calculation. They are the written documents summarizing and reflecting the financial position and operating results of an enterprise, including a balance sheet, an income statement, a cash flow statement together with supporting schedules, notes to the financial statements, and explanatory statements on financial condition.

Financial reports are used to provide the users with useful accounting information related to their decision-making. The users include present and potential investors, creditors, government departments, finance and security institutions, management of a business and others.

In accordance with the requirements of accounting standards for business enterprise, a business would prepare a balance sheet, an income statement, a cash flow statement and other financial reports at the end of a month, a quarter or a year. The preparations of accounting statements must be true in tables, correct in calculation, complete in contents, and issued on time.

A balance sheet is an accounting statement that reflects the financial position of an enterprise at a specific date, and items of the balance sheet should be grouped according to the categories of assets, liabilities and owners' equity and shall be shown item by item.

Table 6-1　Balance Sheet

Assets	Liabilities
Current assets	Current liabilities
Cash and cash equivalents	Short-term borrowings
Trading financial assets	Accounts payable

Assets	Liabilities
Accounts receivable	Received in advance
Notes receivable	Accrued employee compensation
Less: provision for bad debts	Tax payable
Accounts receivable – net value	Other payables
Prepayment	Non-current liabilities due within one year
Other receivable	Total current liabilities
Inventories	
Total current assets	
Non-current assets	Non-current liabilities
Available for sale financial assets	Long-term borrowings
Held to maturity investment	Long-term payables
Long-term equity investment	Special payable
Investment properties	Accrued liabilities
Fixed assets	Deferred tax liabilities
Property, plant and equipment	Total non-current liabilities
Less: accumulated depreciation	
Fixed asset—net value	Equity
Disposal of fixed assets	Share capital
Construction in progress	Capital surplus
Long-term prepaid expenses	Surplus reserves
Deferred tax assets	Undistributed profit
Total non-current assets	Foreign currency translation difference
	Total equity
Total assets	Total equity and liabilities

The fundamental forms of balance sheet include the account form and the report form.

An account form of balance sheet has two sides. The left side shows items of assets, the right side shows items of liabilities and owners' equity. It looks just like a "T" account. The account form of balance sheet is based on the equation stated as "Assets = Liabilities + Owners' Equity" which is shown above.

The report form of the balance sheet states items of assets, liabilities and capital horizontally, where assets are stated on the upper part of the balance sheet, liabilities and owners' equity on the lower part. The report form of balance sheet is based on the equation stated as "Assets – Liabilities = Capital".

6.2   Income Statement

The income statement is an accounting statement that reflects the operating results of an enterprise within an accounting period, as well as the distribution.

Items of the income statement should be arranged according to the formation and distribution of profit, and shall be shown item by item. Items of profit distribution, which is part of the income statement, may be shown separately in a statement of profit distribution.

The purpose of preparing the income statement is to provide users with accounting information on the operating results of the business. Functions of the income statement are as follows:

To help explain, evaluate and predict the operating results and profitability of a business;

To help explain, evaluate and predict solvency;

To help the management make operating decision;

To help evaluate the management's performance.

How to edit the income statement? In fact we should edit the income statement based on the realization concept, the matching concept, recognition of expenses, materiality principle and conservatism principle etc.

Under different methods of calculating net income or loss, the main forms of the income statement include the single-step form and multiple-step form.

6.2.1   Single-Step Form

The single-step income statement means that items of revenues, costs, expenses, and profits are sorted vertically. Then the revenues and expenses are totaled respectively and finally offset to determine the net income or loss of the period.

The statement is simple and convenient to prepare, however, it fails to disclose the relationship between revenues and expenses at different levels, therefore, it is inconvenient to compare and analyze among different periods or different businesses at present, it is mainly adopted by the service business whose transactions are simple in China.

6.2.2   Multiple-Step Income Statement

This method means that the contents of the statement are classified into several medium calculating procedures to compute the net income or loss, so that the specific classified information is obtained. In accordance with the regulations of accounting system in China, this form should be regarded as standard. In China, the basic form of the statement is shown as follows:

Table 6-2   Income Statement

Items	Current period	Current year cumulative
(i)Total operating revenue		
(ii)Total operating cost		
Cost of goods sold		
Taxes and surcharges		
Selling expenses		
General and administrative expenses		
Financial expenses		
Assets impairments loss		
Add: Net gains from changes in fair value		
Investment income		
(iii)Operating profit		
Add: Non-operating income		
Subtract: Non-operating expenses		
(iv)Profit before tax		
Subtract: Income tax		
(v)Net profit		
(vi)Earnings per share		

The multiple-step income statement provides more comprehensive financial information to analyze conveniently formation of profit as well as compare and analyze the operating results in different periods or between different businesses. However, because the matching of current income and expenses is sorted in order deliberately and some medium results are calculated in accordance with such an order on the multiple-step income statement, it may lead to misunderstanding sources of income or loss, meanwhile it is difficult to hold unified views on item classification.

6.3   Cash Flow Statement

When preparing financial statements for external users, business may elect either to prepare a statement of changes in financial position on working capital basis or to prepare a statement of cash flows.

The management of cash flows is a critical function in the operation of a business enterprise. The statement of cash flows may be prepared and used internally as part of the process of planning and controlling cash movements. Cash budgets are important to the management of cash flows. Our focus here, however, is on cash flow statements prepared for external users to the business.

The cash flow statement can be edited based on 3 classifications that are operating activity, investing activity and financing activity.

6.3.1 Structure of the Cash Flow Statement

1. Operating activity

Operating activities include major cash flows such as sale of goods or services and other inflows like interest revenue, etc. Operating activities also include cash outflows such as purchase of inventory, and payment for wages, taxes, interest, rent, utilities, etc. The amounts provided by operating activities are key figures in a statement of cash flow. Please note that although cash flows in the form of interest and dividend might logically be classified as investing activities, the FASB decides to classify them as operating activities, while in China, they are classified as financing activities.

The methods for it can be classified into direct method and indirect method.

With the direct method of reporting cash flows from operating activity, summaries of operating inflows and outflows are shown and then combined to arrive at the net cash flow from operations. It results in a straightforward presentation that is intuitively understandable by users with little or no accounting training. However, it doesn't suggest why the year's net operating cash flow differs from the year's net income. For this reason, the direct method is not the one used by most companies. The direct method shows the major classes of operating cash receipts and cash payments. The difference between cash receipts and payments is the net cash flow provided by operating activities. The direct method is straightforward and is not likely to be misunderstood, so many financial statement users prefer it.

The indirect method which is called reconciliation method, involves reconciling net income reported on the income statement and net cash flow calculated on the statement of cash flows. The approach of the indirect method is to start with the net income amount and adjust it for differences between revenues and operating cash inflows, and for differences between expenses and operating cash outflows. The indirect method is much harder to understand by users than the direct method, but it can help user to understand the reasons for the difference between the period's net income and the period's net cash flow from operation. Essentially, this reconciliation requires adjusting net income for any items that do not affect cash, such as depreciation or amortization, and then adjusting accrual-based account balances to a cash basis. The indirect method produces the same result as the direct method. It is favored and used by most accountants because it is easier to use and it helps explain the reasons for the difference between net income and net cash flow.

Financial accounting standards board issued principle about "statement of cash flows", which was abbreviated as SFAS No.95. It encourages enterprises to report cash flows from operating activity directly by showing major classes of operating cash receipts and payments. Enterprises that choose not to show operating cash receipts and payments are required to report the same amount of net cash flows from operating activities indirectly by adjusting net income to reconcile it to net cash flows from operating activities by removing the effects of (1) all deferrals of past operating cash receipts and payments and all accruals of expected future operating cash receipts and payments and (2) all items that are included in net income but do not affect operating cash receipts and payments. If the direct method is used, a reconciliation of net income and net cash flows from operating activity is required to be provided in a separate schedule.

2. Investing activity

It relates to the purchase of fixed assets, intangibles, and other long-term assets. In addition, investing activities include the purchase and sale of financial instruments not intended for trading purposes, as well as the making and collecting of loans.

3. Financing activity

Financial activities include transactions and events whereby cash is obtained from or repaid to owners and creditors.

Cash flows in a cash flow statement should be classified into three categories: cash flows from operating activities, cash flows from investing activities, and cash flows from financing activities. Each category should be further divided into two parts: cash inflows and outflows. The format of it is as follows:

Table 6-3　Cash Flow Statement

Prepared by:　　　　　　　　　　　　　　　　　　　　　　　　　　　　　Unit:

Items	Line	Amount
CASH FLOWS FROM OPERATING ACTIVITIES	1	
CASH RECEIVED FROM SALES OF GOODS OR RENDERING SERVICE	2	
RETURNING OF TAXATIONS	3	
OTHER CASH RECEIVED RELATING TO OPERATING ACTIVITIES	4	
SUB TOTAL OF CASH INFLOWS	5	
CASH PAID FOR GOODS AND SERVICE	6	
CASH PAID TO AND ON BEHALF OF EMPLOYEES	7	
TAXES PAID	8	
OTHER CASH PAID RELATING TO OPERATING ACTIVITIES	9	
SUB TOTAL OF CASH OUTFLOWS	10	
NET CASH FLOWS FROM OPERATING ACTIVITIES	11	
CASH FLOWS FROM INVESTING ACTIVITIES	12	
PROCEEDS FROM SALES OF NON-DEALING SECURITIES	13	
DIVIDENDS RECEIVED	14	
PROCEEDS FROM THE DISPOSAL OF FIXED ASSETS, INTANGIBLE ASSETS AND OTHER ASSETS	15	

续表

Items	Line	Amount
OTHER PROCEEDS RELATING TO INVESTING ACTIVITIES	16	
SUB TOTAL OF CASH INFLOWS	17	
CASH PAID TO ACQUIRE FIXED ASSETS, INTANGIBLE ASSETS AND OTHER LONG-TERM ASSETS	18	
CASH PAID TO ACQUIRE INVESTMENT	19	
OTHER CASH PAID RELATING TO INVESTMENT ACTIVITIES	20	
SUB TOTAL OF CASH OUTFLOWS	21	
NET CASH FLOWS FROM INVESTING ACTIVITIES	22	
CASH FLOWS FROM INVESTING FINANCING ACTIVITIES	23	
PROCEEDS FORM ISSUING SHARES	24	
PROCEEDS FROM BORROWINGS	25	
OTHER PROCEEDS RELATING TO FINANCING ACTIVITIES	26	
SUB TOTAL OF CASH INFLOWS	27	
CASH PAYMENTS OF DEBT	28	
CASH PAYMENTS OF DIVIDENDS AND PROFIT, INTEREST EXPENSE	29	
OTHER PAYMENTS RELATING TO FINANCING ACTIVITIES	30	
SUB TOTAL OF CASH OUTFLOWS	31	
NET CASH FLOWS FROM FINANCING ACTIVITIES	32	
EFFECT OF FOREIGN EXCHANGE RATE CHARGES ON CASH	33	
NET INCREASE IN CASH AND CASH EQUIVALENTS	34	

6.3.2 Preparing a Complete Statement of Cash Flows

Five steps are generally required in preparing a complete statement of cash flows:

(1) Determine the change in cash and cash equivalents. This is simply the difference between beginning and ending cash balances for the period being analyzed. The cash flow statement is not done until the total cash flow from operating, investing, and financing activity is equal to the net change in cash.

(2) Determine the net cash provided by operating activity. This step requires analysis of each income statement item and the changes in all current operating assets and current operating liabilities.

(3) Determine the net cash provided by investing activity. This step requires analysis of the changes in all non-current assets as well as changes in all non-operating current assets.

(4) Determine the net cash provided by financing activity. This step requires analysis of the changes in all non-current liabilities, all equity accounts and all non-operating current liabilities.

(5) Prepare a formal statement of cash flows, classified according to operating activity,

investing activity and financing activity. Any significant non-cash investing or financing transactions should not be reported in the statement of cash flows but should be disclosed separately.

Key Words and Phrases

cash receipts and payments	现金收入和现金支出
cash equivalent	现金等价物
liquidity	流动性，变现能力
operating, investing and financing activities	经营活动，投资活动，筹资活动
fund	资金
statement of changes in financial position	财务状况变动表
working capital	营运资金
account form	账户式
report form	报告式
operating result	经营结果
profitability	盈利性
single-step form	单步式
multiple-step form	多部式
cash flow statement	现金流量表

Exercises

I. Decide whether each statement is true or false.

1. Balance sheet shows the operating results of the business at the end of the year.　(　　)

2. In the report form, the assets are listed on the left side of the page and liabilities and owners' equity on the right side.　(　　)

3. Balance sheet is a status report.　(　　)

4. Long-lived assets are assets that can be easily converted into cash or used up during the normal operating cycle of the business or within one year.　(　　)

5. Bonds payable is a kind of current liabilities.　(　　)

II. Fill in the blanks.

1. The format of the balance sheet can be subdivided into _____ and _____.

2. The balance sheet shows the _____ of the business at the end of the time period.

3. Assets are further divided into _____ and _____.

4. Liabilities are further subdivided into _____ and _____.

5. The two basic sources of owners' equity are _____ and _____.

6. The format of income statement includes _____ and _____.

7. The income statement describes _____ of a business for a particular accounting period.

8. Operating expenses consist of _____ and _____.

9. _____ activities include the production, _____ and delivery of the company's product as well as collecting payment from its customers.

10. Expense and income must be matched in the same _____.

III. Multiple choices.

1. Which of the following belongs to the current assets? (   ).

   A. Investment   B. Plant and equipment

   C. Intangible assets   D. Inventory

2. Which of the following belongs to the long-term liabilities? (   ).

   A. Retaining earnings   B. Capital stock

   C. Dividends payable   D. Bonds payable

3. Which of the following belongs to owners' equity? (   ).

   A. Prepaid expenses   B. Notes payable

   C. Capital stock   D. Mortgages payable

4. Financial statement does not include_____.

   A. balance sheet   B. income statement

   C. cash flow statement   D. working sheet

5. Which of the following belongs to current liabilities? (   ).

   A. Mortgages payable   B. Prepaid expenses

   C. Notes payable   D. Bonds payable

6. Which of the following belongs to other revenues and gains? (   ).

   A. Sales   B. Interest expense

   C. Intangible assets   D. Dividend revenue

7. Which of the following belongs to other expenses and losses? (   ).

   A. Income from fees   B. Selling expenses

   C. Cost of goods sold   D. Interest expense

8. Which of the following statement is correct? (   ).

   A. The income statement is a status statement.

   B. The multi-step income statement has several significant subtotals.

   C. Advertising expense is a part of general & administrative expenses.

   D. The multiple-step income statement is easier to read than the single-step income statement.

IV. Compute the amount of net income.

1. Sales	$105,000
2. Sales Returns	3,000
3. Sales Discounts	2,000
4. Inventory, Jan, 1	60,000
5. Purchase	33,000
6. Purchase Returns and Allowances	2,000
7. Purchase Discounts	1,000
8. Inventory, Dec, 31	30,000
9. Selling Expenses	20,000
10. General & Administrative	10,000
11. Rent Revenue	1,000
12. Interest Expense	5,000

Here we assume that the rate of income tax expense is 30%.

(1) Compute the amount of cost of goods sold.

(2) Compute the amount of income from operations.

(3) Compute the amount of income tax expense.

(4) Compute the amount of net income.

V. Prepare a balance sheet as of December 31, 2001 from the data below.

Accounts payable	$3,000	Supplies	$ 200
Cash	4,000	Net Income	11,400
Equipment	16,000	Drawing	10,200
Notes Payable	12,000	Capital, January 1, 2001	4,000

Reading Materials

The Three Types of Financial Statements

It has been my experience that all watchful business owners have an innate sense of how well their business is doing. Almost without thinking about it, these business owners can tell you any time during the month how close they are to hitting budgeted figures. Certainly, cash in bank plays a part, but it's more than that. Helpful is the routine review of financial statements. There are three types of financial statements. Each will give you important information about how efficiently and effectively your business is operating.

The first step in learning how to prepare financial statements is understanding the accounting system, which is how you get transactions to show up on the financial statements.

INCOME STATEMENT

The income statement shows all items of income and expense for your arts or crafts business. It reflects a specific time period. So an income statement for the quarter ending March 31 shows revenue and expenses for January, February and March; if the income statement is for the calendar year ending December 31, it would contain all your information from January 1 to December 31.

Income statements are also known as statements of profit and loss or P&Ls. The bottom line on an income statement is income less expenses. If your income is more than expense, you have a net profit. If expense is more than income, you have a net loss.

BALANCE SHEET

Accounting is based upon a double-entry system, for every entry into the books there has to be an opposite and equal entry. The net effect of the entries is zero, which means your books are balanced. The proof of this balancing act is shown in the balance sheet when Assets = Liabilities + Equity.

The balance sheet shows the health of a business from day one to the date on the balance sheet. Balance Sheets are always dated on the last day of the reporting period. If you've been in business since 1997 and your balance sheet is dated as of December 31 of the current year, the balance sheet will show the results of your operations from 1997 to December 31 of the current year.

STATEMENT OF CASH FLOWS

The statement of cash flows shows the ins and outs of cash during the reporting period. You may be thinking that who needs that type of report? I'll just look at the checkbook. Good point, unless you're reporting things that don't immediately affect cash such as depreciation, accounts receivable and accounts payable.

If I could only choose one of those three financial statements to evaluate the ability of a company to pay dividends and meet obligations (indicating a healthy business) I would pick the statement of cash flows. The statement of cash flows takes aspects of the income statement and balance sheet and kind of craming them together to show cash sources and uses for the period.

Part Two

Special Topics of Assets

Chapter 7　Cash and Its Control

After studying this chapter, you should be able to:

- Explain the concept of cash and cash equivalents;
- Describe the transactions about cash receipts and cash payments;
- Understand internal control over cash;
- Explain the concept of petty cash and the operation of the petty cash fund;
- Explain bank statement;
- Understand the need for reconciling the bank balance;
- Prepare bank reconciliation.

7.1　Cash

Liquidity refers to how readily an asset can be converted into other types of assets, or is used to buy services or pay off obligations. **Cash** is a current asset that includes currency, coin, money orders received from customers, amount held in the form of demand deposits, savings accounts, and certificates of deposit. There are examples of liquid assets because they possess the characteristic of convertibility.

Cash equivalents are assets that are readily convertible into cash, such as money market funds, short-term government bonds or treasury bills, marketable securities and commercial paper. Cash equivalents are distinguished from other investments through their short-term existence; they mature within 3 months whereas short-term investments are 12 months or less, and long-term investments are any investments that mature in excess of 12 months. Another important condition a cash equivalent needs to satisfy is that the investment should have insignificant risk of change in value; thus, common stock cannot be considered a cash equivalent, but preferred stock acquired shortly before its redemption date can be.

Cash appears on the balance sheet at its face value. In the case of foreign currency, the amount of foreign currency is translated into domestic currency using the exchange rate on the balance sheet date.

7.2　The Transactions about Cash Receipts and Cash Payments

7.2.1　Cash Receipts

1)　The way of cash receipts

Receipts from credit customers;

Receipts from customers without a credit account.

2)　Relevant supporting information or documents

Supporting documents relate to receipts on sales;

Cash receipts should be separately totaled in notes, coins, cheques, credit and debit card and the amount in bank which is shown in Figure 7-1.

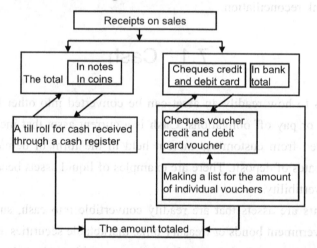

Figure 7-1　The Table of Receipts on Sales

Supporting documents relative to receipts from credit customers are remittance list or cash received list. When money is received from credit customers, it is important to make sure that each receipt is properly recorded. A common method of doing this is to start by preparing *a remittance list or cash received list*. A remittance list is simply a list of each receipt, with details of which the money has come from and the amount of the receipts.

Customer	Account number	Amount received	Settlement discount taken
JACK	1001	1000	10
ROSE	1002	1500	20
MIKE	1003	3000	----

Note:

Settlement discount taken should be checked to make sure that the customer is entitled to the discount and has paid within the required time limit; the amount of the discount has been calculated correctly.

【Example 7.1】

Cabot Wholesale Distribution Company sold merchandise to a manufacture. The invoice price was 1,000 dollars and the credit terms were 3/10, n/60 (the cost of the goods is 600).

Suppose the manufacturer paid within the discount period of 10 days. The seller would record the sale and collection as follows:

Dr. Account receivable   1,000
    Cr. Sales revenue   1,000

To record the cost of goods sold as follows:

Dr. The cost of goods sold   600
    Cr. Inventory   600

To record the collection within the discount period as follows:

Dr. Cash   970
    Sales discounts/ financial expenses   30
    Cr. Account receivable   1,000

When receiving the receipts beyond the limit period, the accounting entry should be as follows:

Dr. Cash   1,000
    Cr. Account receivable   1,000

Receipts matching with the invoice should be audited. When money is received from a credit customer, the receipt should be matched with the invoice that the customer is paying. Sometimes, a customer might pay several invoices at the same time.

7.2.2 Cash Payments

Cash payments is the outflow in the cash flow statement, so it is important to record the cash payments for a company. First we will understand the way for cash payments and then we will grasp the documentation for it.

1) Cash payments

There are two methods for cash payments. The first method is to pay the expenditure when it happened directly. The second method is to be given a limit period. In another word, we can pay within the limit time to utilize the preferential term.

2) The supporting documents

There are various documents on cash payments as follows:

The till on cash register; the voucher from bank; receipts; purchase invoice and other source documents having signatures; check requisitions or expense claim form and a listing of payment.

7.3   Internal Control over Cash

Internal control over cash is sometimes regarded merely as a means of preventing fraud and theft. A good system of internal control, however, will also aid in achieving the other objectives of efficient cash management, including accurate accounting for cash transactions, anticipating the need for borrowing, and the maintenance of adequate but not excessive cash balances. The following internal control procedures should be carefully and consistently followed:

- Responsibility for handling cash and checks (custody) should be separated from the keeping of cash records.
- All cash receipts should be deposited intact each day. This is necessary in order to safeguard assets and maintain adequate records.
- All payments should be made by check. Minor payments are made from a petty cash fund, not from cash receipts.

The petty cash tin is kept in a secure place, such as a locked desk drawer, to deter theft. Only one or possibly two designated individuals should be permitted to make payments from the tin. To reduce the risk of loss, a business should only keep cash in petty cash reasonably necessary, so that if the petty cash tin is stolen, the amount of the loss might not be large.

7.3.1   The Characteristics of an Effective System of Internal Control

Assignment of responsibilities—each employee is assigned certain responsibilities.

Proper authorization—an organization generally has a written set of rules that outlines approved procedures.

Separation of duties—dividing responsibilities for transactions limits the chances for fraud and promotes accuracy of the accounting records. Separation of duties may be divided into four parts:

1. Separation of operations from accounting—the entire accounting function should be completely separated from operating departments.

2. Separation of custody of assets from accounting—accountants should not have access to assets, and those who have access to assets (such as the cashier) should not have access to the accounting records.

3. Separation of authorization of transactions from the custody of related assets—people who authorize transactions should not handle the related asset.

4. Separation of duties within the accounting function—different people should perform the various phrases of accounting to minimize errors and opportunities for fraud.

7.4   Petty Cash Fund

A petty cash fund is established to make small cash payments (for example, taxi fares, postages, express charges, and small supplies), so that cheques need not be written every time.

The practice for petty cash fund includes the following contents.

Establishing the fund

An estimate is made of the total small payment likely to be required during a short period, usually a month. A cheque is written for this amount, cashed, and the money turned over to the staff member in charge of the petty cash fund.

【Example 7.2】Tony established a $500 petty cash fund on April 1.

Dr. Petty cash   500
    Cr. Cash   500

Making petty cash payment

The disbursement of cash from the petty cash fund is usually documented by a petty cash receipt. For purpose of control, the custodian of the fund signs the receipt. The total fund amount in cash and/or petty cash receipts should be known at all times.

Reimbursing the fund

When the money in the petty cash fund reaches a minimum level or at the end of an accounting period, the fund is reimbursed. The receipts and supporting documents are examined in the treasurer's office to verify that they are proper payments from the fund. The treasurer then approves the request and a check is prepared to restore the fund to its established amount. At the same time, all supporting documentation is stamped "paid" so that it can not be submitted again for payment.

We can see the factors on the petty cash day book.

(1) Debit side: amount of increases about petty cash.

(2) Credit side: amount of decreases about petty cash.

【Example 7.3】

On April 30, tony company's fund had $228.50 in cash and receipts for these expenditures: postage expense $24.90, delivery expense $127.10 and repairs expenses $119.50. The fund was reimbursed on April 30.

Dr. Postage expense   24.90
    Delivery expense   127.10
    Repairs expense   119.50
    Cr. Cash in bank   271.50

【Example 7.4】

Suppose that the fund was not only reimbursed on April 30 but also reduced to $400 because it was not being used as frequently as expected. The entry to record this requirement is as follows:

Dr. Postage expense	24.90
Delivery expense	127.10
Repairs expense	119.50
Cr. Petty cash	100
Cash in bank	171.50

7.4.1 The Purpose of Petty Cash

In every business, there will be a number of small expenses that have to be paid for in notes and coins, instead of by cheque or by other methods of payment. To make these payments, a supply of cash has to be kept on the business premises. This cash is called petty cash. The using of petty cash is divided into 3 steps, which are shown in Figure 7-2.

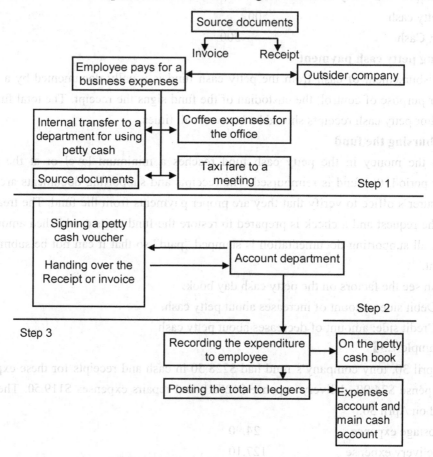

Figure 7-2   The Procedure for Using Petty Cash

7.4.2 Documentation and Authorization

Before using petty cash, we should fill a petty cash voucher. The format of the petty cash voucher is shown in Table 7-1.

Petty cash voucher No._____		
Date_____		
For what required	Amount	
Signature _____		
Authorized _____		

Table 7-1   The Format of the Voucher

In the petty cash voucher, we can see there are main factors. They are date, details for the payment, amount, signature and authorization from a person.

In fact, petty cash is small amount of money kept in an office to pay small debts or expenses. In normal operation, they are recorded in the petty cash book. Petty cash payment is noted in the petty cash book. Of course, they are locked in metal box, in an office. In the metal box, there are petty cash voucher. The voucher is a piece of paper, showing the amount and reason for petty cash expenditure. It is also proved for recording followed.

7.4.3   Accounting System Relative to Cash Book

Firstly, we should record petty cash payments on petty cash book, and then total them. The methods for dealing with petty cash transactions are classified imprest system and non-imprest system.

1. Imprest system

The imprest system is a system, in which there is a maximum amount of money in petty cash, the imprest amount. The imprest amount varies from one organization to another, and might be enough to make petty cash payments for about a special period of two or four weeks. In another word, a petty cash box is started with a certain amount of cash. This amount of cash is known as the imprest amount.

2. Non-imprest system

It is simply to pay a fixed amount of money into petty cash every so often, to top it up.

【Example 7.5】

A management sector of Company Dasheng, which adopts a "non-imprest system" to borrow $1,600 for office supplies, then what is the treatment for the transaction?

The finance department under the original documents for cash payment vouchers, accounts record as:

Debit. Other receivables   1,600

     Credit. Cash   1,600

【Example 7.6】

The expenditure is 1,520 yuan, and then which is record?

Debit. Management expenses	1,520
Cash	80
Credit. Other receivables	1,600

【Example 7.7】

If the actual expenditure is 1,790, and in another word, the document is 1,790, then what is the record?

Debit. Management expense	1,790
Credit. Other receivable	1,600
Cash	190

7.5 Bank Reconciliations

Good internal control practice requires that cash be deposited daily and payment be made by cheque. Banks produce checking account statements, which provide a separate and external record of all cash transactions. This statement can be used to prove the cash balance in the company's own records.

7.5.1 General Bank Service and Operation of Bank Clearing System

Keeping cash in a bank account helps control cash because banks have established practice for safeguarding customer's money. Banks also provide customers with detailed records of their transactions. To take full advantage of the bank, the business should deposit all cash receipts in the bank and make all cash payments through the bank. An exception is a petty cash transaction, which we have introduced above.

The documents used to control a bank account include the following:

Signature card, deposit ticket, check, bank statement and bank reconciliation.

Signature card

Bank requires each person authorized to transact business through an account to sign a signature card. The bank uses the signature card to protect against forgery.

Deposit ticket

Banks supply standard forms such as deposit tickets. The customer fills in the dollar amount of each deposit. As a proof of the transaction, the customer keeps a deposit receipt.

Check

To draw money from an account, the depositor writes a check, which is the document that tells the bank to pay the designated party a specified amount of money. There are three parties to a check; the maker, who signs the check; the payer, to whom the check is paid, and the bank on which the check is drawn.

Source of cash includes cash sales of goods to customers, loans from banks and investments in the business by the owners. Proper management of cash is very important. Internal control must be established to safeguard cash from losses or thief.

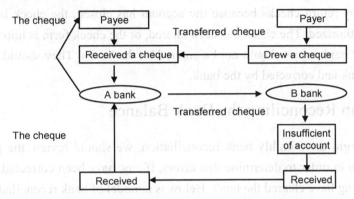

Figure 7-3   The Procedure for Drawing Money

7.5.2   Reconciling the Bank Balance

Usually the balance of the bank statement and the balance of the depositor's account will not agree. The differences are caused by errors or time differences. Errors occur because the bank and depositor may make mistakes in the amount, or an amount may be posted to the wrong account. These errors must be corrected. Any transactions recorded by the bank but not yet entered on the company's books should be promptly recorded. The reconciling items will fall into two broad groups: (1) those on the depositor's books but not recorded by the bank; (2) those on the bank statement but not on the books.

(1)   Items on books but not on bank statement.

Deposit in transit: money that has been deposited by the company but not yet recorded by the bank.

Outstanding checks: checks that have been issued by the company but not yet paid by the bank.

Bookkeeping errors: errors in recording amounts of checks.

(2)   Items on bank statement but not on books.

Bank collections: money collected by the bank on behalf of its customers. Some companies use a lock-box system where customers make payments directly to reduce theft.

Electronic funds transfer (EFT): the bank statement may include EFT that the company has not yet recorded.

Service charges: fees that the bank charges for certain services and are not known by the depositor until the bank statement is received.

Interest revenue earned on the checking account: the amount of interest earned may not be known until the bank statement is received.

Non-sufficient funds checks (NSF): NSF checks received from customers and returned to the payee, they are sometimes included in the bank statement.

Checks collected, deposited, and returned to payee by the bank for reasons other than NSF: the bank may return checks because the account has closed, the check is too old, and the signature is not authorized. The check has been altered, or the check form is improper.

Bank errors: bank errors should not be entered on the books. They should be brought to the attention of the bank and corrected by the bank.

7.5.3 Steps in Reconciling the Bank Balance

Before we begin the monthly bank reconciliation, we should review the previous month's bank reconciliation in order to determine that errors, if any, have been corrected and that items in transit or outstanding have cleared the bank. Below is a model of bank reconciliation.

Figure 7-4 Bank Reconciliation Form

Xxx company Bank Reconciliation
April 1, 20xx

Bank statement balance	$xx	Book balance of cash	$xx
Deposit in transit	xx	Bank collections	xx
		Interest revenue earned	xx
	xx		xx
Less:		Less:	
Outstanding checks	xx	NSF check	xx
		Bank service charge	xx
	xx		xx
Reconciled balance	xx	Reconciled balance	xx

The final amounts should agree. If these final amounts do not agree, we must look carefully for reconciling items omitted from the schedule or for possible errors in record keeping.

【Example 7.8】 B Company deposits all receipts intact on the day received and makes all payments by checks. On July 31, 2010, after all posting was completed; the company's cash account showed a $1,133 debit balance. However, B company's July 31 bank statement showed $1,330 on deposit in the bank on that day. From both B company's records and the July bank statement, the following information is available:

- Outstanding checks, $ 702.
- $ 18 debit memorandum for bank service.
- Check #20 was correctly drawn for $ 489 in payment of the utility bill and was paid by the bank on July 15. However, it had been recorded with a debit to utilities expense and

a credit to cash as though it were for $498.

- The July 31 cash receipts, $496, were placed in the bank's night depository after banking hours on that date and were recorded by the bank at the time the July bank statement was prepared.

Required: prepare bank reconciliation.

B Company

Bank reconciliation

July 31, 2017

Bank statement balance	$1,330	Book balance of cash	$1,133
Add:		Add:	
Deposit of July 31	496	Error on Ch. #20	9
Total	1,826	Total	1,142
Deduct:		Deduct:	
Outstanding checks	702	Bank service charge	18
Reconciled balance	$1,124	Reconciled balance	$1,124

Key Words and Phrases

liquidity	流动性
cash	现金
cash equivalent	现金等价物
commercial paper	商业票据
treasury bills	国库券
internal controls	内部控制
petty cash fund	备用金
bank reconciliation	银行余额调节表
bank statement	银行对账单
cancelled checks	已注销的支票
credit memorandum	贷项通知单
debit memorandum	借项通知单
deposit in transit	在途存款
drawee	付款人，受票人
drawer	开票人
electronic funds transfer	电子资金转账
non-sufficient funds checks	存款不足支票
outstanding checks	未兑现支票
service charge	手续费

Exercises

I. Decide whether each statement is true or false.

1. An electronic funds transfer is a system that transfers cash by electronic communication rather than by paper documents. ( )

2. The initial entry to establish a petty cash fund involves a debit to cash and a credit to petty cash. ( )

3. A bank reconciliation explains the effects of all cash receipts and all cash made through the bank. ( )

4. That have been issued by the company but not yet paid by the bank are called outstanding checks. ( )

5. The differences between bank balance with book balance are caused by errors or timing differences. ( )

II. Fill in the blanks.

1. At least once a month, bank provides a _____ to each client which shows the cash disbursements, cash deposits, and their effects on the balance of cash account as recorded by the bank.

2. Money that has been deposited by the company but not yet recorded by the bank is called _____.

3. NSF checks received from customers and returned to the payee, they are sometimes included in the _____.

4. _____ can show companies' bank transactions and balances and be used to prove the cash balance in the company's own records.

5. In reconciling the bank account, it is customary to reconcile the balance per books and balance per bank to their_____.

III. Multiple choices.

1. The three parties to a check are the _____.
   A. bank, payee, and the IRS   B. bank, maker, and payer
   C. signer, depositor, and endorser D. maker, payee, and bank

2. Cash is shown on a balance sheet as a _____.
   A. long-term investment   B. long-term asset
   C. current asset   D. long-term liability

3. Cash equivalents include_____.
   A. time deposits   B. inventories
   C. accounts receivable   D. prepaid expenses

4. A fund containing a small amount of cash that is used to pay for minor expenditures is known as a(n)_____.

    A. expenditure fund   B. expense fund

    C. petty cash fund   D. payments fund

5. The entry to reimburse the petty cash fund includes a _____.

    A. credit to petty cash   B. debit to cash in bank

    C. debit to various expenses and assets   D. debit to petty cash

6. Controls over petty cash include all of the following except_____.

    A. support all petty cash payments with a petty cash ticket

    B. designate several employees as petty cash custodians

    C. keep a specific amount of cash on hand

    D. all of the above represent controls over petty cash

IV. Finish the following task.

From the following data, prepare a bank reconciliation for the company.

Laird Company deposits all receipts intact on the day received and makes all payment by check. On April 30, 2006, after all posting was completed; the company's cash account showed an $21,589.45 debit balance. However, Laird Company's April 30 bank statement showed $25,907.45 on deposit in the bank on that day. From both Laird company's records and the April bank statement, the following reconciling items are determined:

1. Deposits in transit: April 30 deposit (received by bank on May 1) $2201.40

2. Outstanding checks: No. 453 $3,000;

                  No. 457 $1,401.30;

                  No. 459 $1,502.70

3. Errors: check No. 443 was correctly written by Laird for $1,226 and was correctly paid by the bank. However, it was recorded for $1,262 by Laird Company.

4. Bank memorandum:

    Debit: bank service fee $455.60

    Credit: collection of note receivable for $1,000 plus interest earned $50, less bank collection fee $15

Reading Materials

The Result of Labor Market Problems

How many people really suffer as a result of labor market problems? This is one of the most critical yet contentious social policy questions. In many ways, our social statistics exaggerate the degree of hardship. Unemployment does not have the same dire consequences today as it did in the 1930's when most of the unemployed were primary breadwinners, when incomes and earnings were usually much closer to the margin of subsistence, and when there were no countervailing social programs for those failing in the labor market. Increasing affluence, the rise of families with more than one wage earner, the growing predominance of secondary earners among the unemployed, and improved social welfare protection have unquestionably mitigated the consequences of joblessness.

Earnings and income data also overstate the dimensions of hardship. Among the millions with hourly earnings at or below the minimum wage level, the overwhelming majority are from multiple earners, relatively affluent families.

Most of those counted by the poverty statistics are elderly or handicapped or have family responsibilities which keep them out of the labor force, so the poverty statistics are by no means an accurate indicator of labor market pathologies.

Yet, there are also many ways for our social statistics to underestimate the degree of labor-market-related hardship. The unemployment counts exclude the millions of fully employed workers whose wages are so low that their families remain in poverty. Low wages and repeated or prolonged unemployment frequently interact to undermine the capacity for self-support. Since the number experiencing joblessness at some time during the year is several times the number unemployed in any month, those who suffer as a result of forced idleness can equal or exceed average annual unemployment, even though only a minority of the jobless in any month really suffer.

For every person counted in the monthly unemployment tallies, there is another working part-time, because of the inability to find full-time work, or else outside the labor force but wanting a job. Finally, income transfers in our country have always focused on the elderly, disabled, and dependent, neglecting the needs of the working poor, so that the dramatic expansion of cash and unkind transfers does not necessarily mean that those failing in the labor market are adequately protected.

As a result of such contradictory evidence, it is uncertain whether those suffering seriously as a result of thousands of the tens of millions, and, hence, whether high levels of joblessness can be tolerated or must be counted by job creation and economic stimulus. This is only one area of agreement in this debate—that the existing poverty, employment, and earnings statistics are inadequate for one of their primary applications, measuring the consequences of labor market problems.

Quiz 4

1. Your cashbook on 31 December 2003 shows a bank balance of 565 overdrawn. On comparing this with your bank statement at the same date, you discover the following.

(1) A cheque for 57 drawn by you on 29 December 2003 has not yet been presented for payment.

(2) A cheque for 92 from a customer, which was paid into the bank on 24 December 2003,

has been dishonored on 31 December 2003.

The correct bank balance to be shown in the balance sheet on 31 December 2003 is (   ).

     A. 714 overdrawn   B. 657 overdrawn

     C. 473 overdrawn   D. 53 overdrawn

2. The cash book shows a bank balance of 5,675 overdrawn on 31 August 2005. It is subsequently discovered that a standing order of 15 has been entered twice, and that a dishonored cheque for 450 has been debited in the cash book instead of credited.

The correct bank balance should be (   ).

     A. 5,100 overdrawn   B. 6,000 overdrawn

     C. 6,250 overdrawn   D. 6,450 overdrawn

3. A business had a balance at the bank of 2,500 at the start of the month. During the following month, it paid for the materials invoiced at 1000 less trade discount of 20% and cash discount of 10%. It received a cheque from a receivable in respect of an invoice for 200, subject to cash discount of 5%.

The balance at the bank at the end of the month was (   ).

     A. 1,970   B. 1,980   C. 1,990   D. 2,000

4. The bank statement on 31 October 2007 showed an overdraft of 800. On reconciling the bank statement, it was discovered that a cheque drawn by your company for 80 had not been presented for payment and that a cheque for 130 from a customer had been dishonored on 30 October 2007.

The correct bank balance to be shown in the balance sheet on 31 October 2007 is (   ).

     A. 1010 overdrawn   B. 880 overdrawn

     C. 750 overdrawn   D. 720 overdrawn

5. Which of the following is not a valid reason for the cash book and bank statement falling to agree? (   ).

     A. Timing difference   B. Bank charges

     C. Error   D. Cash receipts posted to payables

6. A debit entry on a bank statement will have which effect on the level of a bank overdraft and a bank balances? (   ).

Bank Overdraft	Bank Balance
A. increase	increase
B. decrease	decrease
C. increase	decrease
D. decrease	increase

7. When preparing a bank reconciliation, it is realized that:

(1) Cheques with a value of 1,050 have been sent to suppliers and correctly entered in the cash book but have not yet been presented for payment;

(2) A cheque for 75 sent to a supplier has been incorrectly recorded in the cash book as 57;

(3) Before correction the cash book has a balance of 10,500 credit;

(4) Bank charges of 175 have not been recorded in the cash book.

The balance of the cash book after the correction is (　　).

　　A. 10,307 overdrawn　　　　　　　　B. 10,343 overdrawn

　　C. 10,657 overdrawn　　　　　　　　D. 10,693 overdrawn

8. When preparing a bank reconciliation, it is realized that:

(1) Cheques with a value of 1,050 have been sent to suppliers and correctly entered in the cash book but have not yet been presented for payment;

(2) A cheque for 75 sent to a supplier has been incorrectly recorded in the cash book as 57;

(3) Before correction the cash book has a balance of 10,500 credit;

(4) Bank charges of 175 have not been recorded in the cash book.

What is the closing balance shown on the bank statement? (　　).

　　A. 9,257 overdrawn　　　　　　　　B. 9,643 overdrawn

　　C. 11,357 overdrawn　　　　　　　　D. 11,743 overdrawn

9. When preparing bank reconciliation, it is realized that:

(1) There are some presented cheques of 8,000.

(2) There are lodgments of 5,000 uncleared.

(3) Bank charges of 67 have not been recorded in the cash book.

What adjustment should be required to the cash account? (　　).

　　A. Debit 67　　　　B. Credit 67　　　　C. Debit 3067　　　　D. Credit 3067

10. A company uses the imprest system to control its petty cash, keeping a float of 50, since the cash was last replenished it had the following transactions:

(1) 12.5 to the milkman;

(2) 10.00 on taxis;

(3) 5.7 on stationary;

(4) 20 asvance taken by the director for a taxi fare last week returned unused;

(5) 18.5 to the cleaner;

(6) 15 advance to the secretary.

How much should now be drawn out of the bank? (　　).

　　A. 50　　　　　　B. 41.7　　　　　　C. 46.7　　　　　　D. 31.7

11. From the following information, calculate the value of purchases. (　　).

Opening payable	142,600
Cash paid	542,300
Discounts received	13,200
Goods returned	27,500
Closing payables	137,800

　　A. 302,600　　　　B. 506,400　　　　C. 523,200　　　　D. 578,200

12. These figures are related to receivables:

Balance at 1/1/x1	2,500
Balance at 31/12/x1	2,000
Cash from receivables	10,600
Contra with payables ledger	5,000
Increase in allowance for receivables	

What were sales during the year? (   ).
    A. 5,100   B. 14,520   C. 15,100   D. 15,680

13. A purchase invoice shows 10 items priced at 120 less trade discount 20%. A cash discount of 2.5% is allowed if settlement is made within the allowed credit period. How much will be paid if the cash discount applies? (   ).
    A. 1,170   B. 1,200   C. 936   D. 960

14. A receivables control account had a closing balance of 8,500. It contained a contra to the payables control account of 400, but this had been entered on the wrong side of the control account.

The correct balance on the control account should be (   ).
    A. 7,700 debit   B. 8,100 debit   C. 8,400 debit   D. 8,900 debit

15. The debit side of a trial balance totals 50 more than the credit side. This could be due to (   )
    A. a purchase of goods for 50 being omitted from the payables account
    B. a sale of goods for 50 being omitted from the receivables account
    C. an invoice of 25 for electricity being credited to the electricity account
    D. a receipt for 50 from a receivable being omitted from the cash book.

16. Your payables control account has a balance at 1 October 2008 of 34500 credits. During October, credit purchases were 2,400 and payments made to suppliers, excluding cash purchases, and after deducting cash discounts of 1,200 were 68,900. Purchase returns were 4,700.

The closing balance was (   ).
    A. 38,100   B. 40,500   C. 47,500   D. 49,900

Chapter 8　Inventories

After studying this chapter, you should be able to:

- Describe the nature of inventory and determine what goods are included in inventory;
- Understand and distinguish the perpetual inventory system and the periodic inventory system;
- Understand inventory costing methods: FIFO, LIFO, the weighted-average method;
- Compare FIFO, LIFO and the weighted-average method.

8.1　Inventory

In a merchandising company, inventory consists of all goods owned and held for sale to customers. Inventory is converted into cash within the company's operating cycle and therefore, is regarded as a current asset. In the balance sheet, inventory is listed immediately after accounts receivable, because it is just one step further removed from conversion into cash than customer receivables.

A merchandiser (wholesale or retail) will purchase goods from various suppliers for resale. This kind of inventory can be labeled as merchandise inventory.

A manufacturer purchases raw materials and converts them into finished products that are ready for sale. Consequently, a manufacturing concern has three different inventory accounts: raw material inventory; work-in-process inventory; and finished goods inventory.

In general, inventory cost is measured by the total cash equivalent outlay made to acquire the goods and prepare them for sale, or for a service company, to fulfill the requirements of the service contract. The cost of inventory includes all expenditures made in bringing the goods or assets to their existing condition and location for sale. Inventory cost therefore equals invoice price less discounts, plus transportation, storage, insurance, and other costs of preparing the inventory for sale.

8.2　Periodic and Perpetual Inventory System

There are two basic systems used in inventory accounting: periodic and perpetual. The names of the systems indicate the frequency with which inventory quantities are determined.

8.2.1 Periodic Inventory System

A business entity using a periodic inventory system does not maintain a detailed record of each inventory transaction. The purchases of inventory are recorded in the accounting records, just as they are under the perpetual inventory system. However, when sales of inventory are made, only the sales revenue entry is made. There is no entry made to reduce the inventory account and to record cost of goods sold. That means that the inventory account is not up to date during the period since it only records the opening balance and purchases of inventory, but not the consumption of inventory. At the end of the period, a physical count of inventories is taken to arrive at the ending inventory in units and dollars.

The calculation of the cost of goods sold under the periodic inventory system is:

Beginning inventory + Purchases = Cost of goods available for sale

Cost of goods available for sale − Ending inventory = Cost of goods sold

For example, Milagro Corporation has beginning inventory of $100,000, has paid $170,000 for purchases, and its physical inventory count reveals an ending inventory cost of $80,000. The calculation of its cost of goods sold is:

$100,000 Beginning inventory + $170,000 Purchases − $80,000 Ending inventory

= $190,000 Cost of goods sold

8.2.2 Perpetual Inventory System

In a perpetual inventory system, each receipt and each issue of an inventory item is recorded in the inventory records to maintain an up-to-date perpetual inventory balance at all times. The result of the perpetual system is verified at least once a year by physically counting the inventory and matching the count to the accounting records. Thus, the perpetual inventory records provide the units and costs of inventory and cost of goods sold at any time. The unit costs applied to each issue or sale is determined by the cost flow assumption used.

8.2.3 Differences between Perpetual and Periodic System

Following are the main differences between perpetual and periodic inventory systems:

Inventory Account and Cost of Goods Sold Account are used in both systems but they are updated continuously during the period in perpetual inventory system whereas in periodic inventory system they are updated only at the end of the period.

Purchases Account and Purchase Returns and Allowances Account are only used in periodic inventory system and are updated continuously. In perpetual inventory system purchases are directly debited to inventory account and purchase returns are directly credited to inventory account.

Sale Transaction is recorded via two journal entries in perpetual system. One of them records the sale value of inventory whereas the other records cost of goods sold. In periodic inventory system, only one entry is made.

Closing Entries are only required in periodic inventory system to update inventory and cost of goods sold. Perpetual inventory system does not require closing entries for inventory account.

【Example 8.1】

● A company had the following transactions during the current year.

Beginning inventory   100 units at $6 = $600

Purchases   900 units at $6 = $5,400

Sales   600 units at $12 = $7,200

Ending inventory   400 units at $6 = $2,400

● The entries to record these transactions during the current year are shown below:

Perpetual Inventory System		Periodic Inventory System	
1. Beginning inventory, 100 units at $6:		**1. Beginning inventory, 100 units at $6:**	
The inventory account shows the inventory on hand at $600		The inventory account shows the inventory on hand at $600	
2. Purchase 900 units at $6:		**2. Purchase 900 units at $6:**	
Inventory	5,400	Purchases	5,400
Accounts payable	5,400	Accounts payable	5,400
3. Sale of 600 units at $12:		**3. Sale of 600 units at $12:**	
Accounts receivable	7,200	Accounts receivable	7,200
Sales	7,200	Sales	7,200
Cost of goods sold	3,600		--
Inventory	3,600	No Entry	--
4. End of Period Entries for Inventory Accounts:		**4. End of Period Entries for Inventory Accounts:**	
	--	Inventory (Ending by count)	2,400
	--	Cost of goods sold	3,600
No entry necessary	--	Purchases	5,400
	--	Inventory (beginning)	600

8.3 Inventory Costing Methods

Companies face price increases during periods of inflation. To measure inventory amounts during such periods, the accounting profession has developed several costing methods.

Measuring the cost of inventory is easy when prices are constant. But the unit cost often changes. To compute ending inventory and cost of goods sold, the business must assign a cost to each item. The four costing methods are: (1) specific identification; (2) first-in, first-out (FIFO) method; (3) the weighted-average cost; (4) last-in, first-out (LIFO) method.

8.3.1 Specific Identification

The specific identification inventory costing method requires the recording of detailed information for each purchase transaction so that merchandise on hand at the end of an accounting period can be identified with a specific order. Each purchase may be assigned a special number, or a special tag may be placed on each specific order so that each sale can be identified to the related invoice. In this case, the merchandise on hand may be obtained from the purchase invoice. Some businesses deal in items that differ from unit to unit, such as automobiles, jewels, and real estate. There are two reasons why the automotive dealers use the specific cost method. First, the dealer's specific cost is an important determinant of the sales prices. Second, each car is unique, and the serial number links it to a specific invoice cost.

8.3.2 First-in, First-out (FIFO)

The first-in, first-out method, which is often referred to as FIFO, is based upon the assumption that first merchandise acquired is the first merchandise sold. Each sale is made out of the older goods in stock; the ending inventory therefore consists of the most recently acquired goods. In other words, the goods sold or issued are valued at the oldest unit costs, and the goods remaining in inventory are valued at the most recent unit cost amounts. There are two common reasons for the use of FIFO: First, FIFO approximates the physical flow of merchandise and materials. Generally speaking, items that are purchased first are sold first or used first in operations. Second, under historical cost accounting, costs should be matched to revenue in historical sequence—the cost first incurred should be the first that are matched to revenues.

The FIFO method of determining inventory cost may be adopted by any business, regardless of whether or not the physical flow of merchandise actually corresponds to this assumption of selling the oldest units in stock.

Now let's see how to compute ending inventory amounts and the cost of goods sold under FIFO methods. We use the following transaction data to illustrate.

Purchase date	Quantity	Unit price	Total
Jan.1	50	$6.00	$300
Mar. 3	200	$6.50	$1,300
Jun. 6	200	$6.25	$1,250
Sept.10	50	$6.60	$330
	500		$3,180

During the year, 440 units of merchandise were sold and 60 units were on hand at the end of the year.

The ending inventory by FIFO method = $50 \times 6.6 + 10 \times 6.25 = \$392.5$

Cost of goods sold = $50 \times 6.00 + 200 \times 6.50 + 190 \times 6.25 = \$2787.5$

8.3.3 Last-in, First-out (LIFO)

The last-in, first-out (LIFO) method of inventory valuation assumes that the last goods purchased are the first ones sold. The goods that remain unsold at the end of the period would consist of goods in the beginning inventory or the first goods purchased. When using the LIFO inventory pricing method, the first items purchased are assumed to be the last items sold; therefore, the ending inventory would be valued at the earliest or first purchase price.

When prices are rising, LIFO results in lower reported income and thus may provide a related tax benefit. LIFO better matches current costs against current revenues because the most recent purchases are reflected as cost of goods sold. However, it consequently processes the ending inventory at the older, less realistic unit price. Because of this, the LIFO inventory figures on the balance sheet often become quite meaningless in terms of current cost prices.

Let's see how to compute ending inventory amounts and the cost of goods sold under LIFO methods.

Purchase date	Quantity	Unit price	Total
Jan.1	50	$6.00	$300
Mar. 3	200	$6.50	$1,300
Jun. 6	200	$6.25	$1,250
Sept.10	50	$6.60	$330
	500		$3,180

During the year, 440 units of merchandise were sold and 60 units were on hand at the end of the year.

The ending inventory by LIFO method = $50 \times 6.00 + 10 \times 6.50 = \$365$

Cost of goods sold = $50 \times 6.60 + 200 \times 6.25 + 190 \times 6.50 = \$2815$

8.3.4   The Weighted-average Method

The weighted-average method of valuing inventory recognizes that prices will vary as merchandise is purchased during the fiscal period. Therefore, under this method the units in the ending inventory are priced at the average unit cost of the merchandise on hand during the entire fiscal period. Before computing the value of the ending inventory using the weighted average method, the average cost for one unit must be obtained and then applied to the number of units in the ending inventory.

Let's see how to compute the ending inventory amounts and the cost of goods sold under weighted-average methods.

Purchase date	Quantity	Unit price	Total
Jan.1	50	$6.00	$300
Mar. 3	200	$6.50	$1,300
Jun. 6	200	$6.25	$1,250
Sept.10	50	$6.60	$330
	500		$3,180

During the year, 440 units of merchandise were sold and 60 units were on hand at the end of the year.

Average unit cost = $3180 total cost ÷ 500 units purchased = $6.36

The ending inventory = 60 × 6.36 = $381.6

Cost of goods sold = 440 × 6.36 = $2798.4

8.4   Comparing FIFO, LIFO and Average Cost

FIFO produces the lowest cost of goods sold and the highest gross profit. Net income is also the highest under FIFO when inventory costs are rising. Many companies wish to report high income in order to attract investors and borrow on good terms. FIFO offers this benefit.

LIFO results in the highest cost of goods sold and the lowest gross profit. That makes companies pay the lowest income taxes when the inventory costs are rising. Low tax payments conserve a company's cash, but the downside of LIFO is that the company reports low net income.

The average-cost method generates gross profit, income tax, and net income amounts that fall between the extremes of FIFO and LIFO.

Table 8-1   Comparative Results for FIFO, LIFO and Average Cost

	FIFO	LIFO	Average
Sales revenue	$3080	$3080	$3080
Cost of goods sold	2787.5	2815	2798.4
Gross profit	292.5	265	281.6

Key Words and Phrases

inventory	存货
raw materials	原材料
work in process	在产品
finished goods	产成品
periodic inventory system	定期盘存制
perpetual inventory system	永续盘存制
ending inventory	期末存货
specific identification	个别计价法
first-in, first-out (FIFO) cost	先进先出法
weighted-average cost	平均成本法
last-in, first-out (LIFO) cost	后进先出法
cost of goods sold	已销商品成本
gross profit	毛利

Exercises

I. Decide whether each statement is true or false.

1. FIFO and LIFO inventory costing methods are exact opposites of each other.   (   )

2. If a perpetual inventory system is used, cost of goods sold appears on the balance sheet.

(   )

3. Under the FIFO method, ending inventory is valued based on the oldest purchases. (   )

4. When prices are rising, LIFO generally results in the lowest taxable income, and therefore helps reduce tax paid.   (   )

5. FIFO will report the lowest cost of goods sold on the income statement when prices are falling.   (   )

6. When prices are falling, the LIFO method results in the lowest taxable income and thus the lowest income taxes.   (   )

II. Multiple choices.

1. The following units of a particular commodity were available for sale during the period:

beginning inventory.......................40 units at 20

first purchase.............................50 units at 21

second purchase.........................50 units at 22

third purchase............................50 units at 23

What is the unit cost of the 35 units on hand at the end of the period as determined under the periodic system by the FIFO costing method? _____.

  A. 20   B. 21   C. 22   D. 23

2. If merchandise inventory is being valued at cost and the price level is steadily rising, the method of costing that will yield the largest net income is _____.

  A. LIFO   B.FIFO   C. average   D. periodic

3. Inventory is classified as a _____.

  A. fixed asset on the balance sheet

  B. current asset on the balance sheet

  C. current liability on the balance sheet

  D. as either an investment or a current asset on the balance sheet

4. The inventory system that continually discloses the amount of inventory on hand is called_____.

  A. perpetual   B. periodic   C. physical   D. specific identification

5. Refer to the table below and finish the following tasks.

Table

Assume the following data for Burnette company for 20×5:

Beginning inventory		10 units at $7 each
March 18	purchase	15 units at $9 each
April 5	sale	12 units
June 10	purchase	20 units at $10 each
September 15	sale	30 units
October 30	purchase	12 units at $11 each

a. Under the perpetual LIFO method, ending inventory would be valued at _____.

  A. $165   B. $105   C. $153   D. $135

b. Under the perpetual FIFO method, cost of goods sold on the income statement would be_____.

  A. $294   B. $375   C. $462   D. $420

c. Under the perpetual LIFO method, cost of goods sold on the income statement would be _____.

A. $384   B. $294   C. $389   D. $420

6. Which of the following inventory costing methods requires a company to keep track of the actual movement of individual inventory items? _____.

A. LIFO   B. The weighted-average

C. FIFO   D. Specific identification

III. Fill in the blanks.

1. According to GAAP, inventory should be valued on the basis of _____.

2. There are two basis system used in inventory accounting: _____ and _____.

3. A manufacturing concern has three different inventory accounts: _____, _____ and _____.

4. The major inventory costing methods are: _____, _____ and _____.

5. The _____ assumes that goods are used in the order in which they are purchased.

IV. Computation.

1. The beginning inventory and the purchases of commodity during the year were as follows:

Jan. 1 inventory……………………....10 units at 135

Mar.17 purchases…………………..…...20 units at 141

July 2 purchases…………………....…...20 units at 145

Oct.30 purchases……………………....15 units at 144

There are 18 units of the commodity in the physical inventory on December 31 (the perpetual system is used). Determine the inventory cost and the cost of merchandise sold by three methods, presenting your answers in the following form:

Ending inventory   Cost of goods sold

① FIFO

② LIFO

③ average cost

2. Beginning inventory, purchases, and sales data for the commodity in May are as follows:

Inventory, May 1 …………………………20 units at 30

Sales,   May 7…………………..….………....6 units

May 15……………………………….12 units

May 25………………………………….5 units

Purchases, May 4…………………………10 units at 31

May 22………………………....3 units at 33

Assuming that the perpetual inventory system is used, costing by the LIFO method; determine the cost of the inventory balance on May 31.

3. The following data are available for the month of March.

March 1 balance   20 units at $15 each

March 10 purchase   40 units at $16 each

March 17 purchase   30 units at $17.5 each

March 30 purchase   25 units at $18 each

On March 31, 35 units are on hand.

Required: calculate cost of goods sold under the following methods:

A. FIFO

B. LIFO

C. The weighted-average

Reading Materials

Accounting for Inventory

Each country has its own rules about accounting for inventory that fit with their financial-reporting rules. For example, organizations in the U.S. define **inventory** to suit their needs within US Generally Accepted Accounting Practices (GAAP), the rules defined by the Financial Accounting Standards Board (FASB) (and others) and enforced by the U.S. Securities and Exchange Commission (SEC) and other federal and state agencies. Other countries often have similar arrangements but with their own accounting standards and national agencies instead. It is intentional that financial accounting uses standards that allow the public to compare firms' performance, cost accounting functions internally to an organization and potentially with much greater flexibility. A discussion of inventory from standard and Theory of Constraints-based (throughput) cost accounting perspective follows some examples and a discussion of inventory from a financial accounting perspective. The internal costing/valuation of inventory can be complex. Whereas in the past most enterprises ran simple, one-process factories, such enterprises are quite probably in the minority in the 21st century. Where 'one process' factories exist, there is a market for the goods created, which establishes an independent market value for the goods. Today, with multistage-process companies, there is much inventory that would once have been finished goods which is now held as 'work in process' (WIP). This needs to be valued in the accounts, but the valuation is a management decision since there is no market for the partially finished product. This somewhat arbitrary 'valuation' of WIP combined with the allocation of overheads to it has led to some unintended and undesirable results.

Role of Inventory Accounting

By helping the organization to make better decisions, the accountants can help the public sector to change in a very positive way that delivers increased value for the taxpayer's investment. It can also help incentive's progress and ensure that reforms are sustainable and effective in the long term, by ensuring that success is appropriately recognized in both the formal and informal reward systems of the organization. To say that they have a key role to play is an understatement. Finance is connected to most, if not all, of the key business processes within the organization. It should steer the stewardship and accountability systems that ensure that the organization is conducting its business in an appropriate, ethical manner. It is critical that these foundations are firmly laid. So often they are the litmus test by which public confidence in the institution is either won or lost. Finance should also be providing the information, analysis and advice to enable the organizations' service managers to operate effectively. This goes beyond the traditional preoccupation with budgets – how much have we spent so far, how much do we have left to spend? It is about helping the organization to better understand its own performance. That means making the connections and understanding the relationships between given inputs – the resources brought to bear – and the outputs and outcomes that they achieve. It is also about understanding and actively managing risks within the organization and its activities.

FIFO vs. LIFO Accounting

When a merchant buys goods from inventory, the value of the inventory account is reduced by the cost of goods sold (COGS). This is simple where the cost has not varied across those held in stock; but where it has, then an agreed method must be derived to evaluate it. For commodity items that one cannot track individually, accountants must choose a method that fits the nature of the sale. Two popular methods in use are: FIFO (first in-first out) and LIFO (last in-first out). FIFO treats the first unit that arrived in inventory as the first one sold. LIFO considers the last unit arriving in inventory as the first one sold, which method an accountant selects can have a significant effect on net income and book value and, in turn, on taxation. Using LIFO accounting for inventory, a company generally reports lower net income and lower book value, due to the effects of inflation. This generally results in lower taxation. Due to LIFO's potential to skew inventory value, UK GAAP and IAS have effectively banned LIFO inventory accounting. LIFO accounting is permitted in the United States subject to section 472 of the Internal Revenue Code.

Chapter 9　Receivables

After studying this chapter, you should be able to:

- Explain the notes receivable and promissory note;
- Understand how to compute the maturity date and maturity value;
- Understand the process of recording estimated uncollectible accounts;
- Explain how to match bad debt expenses with sales;
- Describe the allowance method of accounting for bad debt.

9.1　Notes Receivable

Another liquid asset is notes receivable. Notes are normally expected to be matured within six months in China. So in published financial statement, notes receivable are often reported in the current asset section of the balance sheet directly after trading securities and before accounts receivable.

Creditor prefers notes receivable (written promise) to accounts receivable (oral promise) for the following reasons:

- Notes may be readily sold to a bank;
- In the event of a lawsuit, a note is a written acknowledgement of the debt and its amount;
- Notes generally earn interest.

A promissory note is an unconditional promise to pay a definite sum of money on demand or at a future date. It contains the following information, as shown in Figure 9-1.

$2,000　　　　　　　　Madison, Wisconsin　　　　　　May 3,20×0

sixty days　　　　　　　　after date _____I_____ promise to pay to

The order of_____Robert Ward_____

Two Thousand and no/100···dollars

For value received with interest at 9%

Payable at First National Bank, Madison

　　　　　　　　　　　　　　　　　　　　　　　　　　　　　　James E. Pott

Figure　9-1

A Promissory Note

(1) Face or principal—the amount of the note;

(2) Date of the note—date note was written;

(3) Term period—time allowed for payment;

(4) Payee—individual to whom payment must be made;

(5) Interest—percentage of annual interest;

(6) Maturity date—date the note is to be paid;

(7) Maker—person liable for payment of the note.

9.1.1 Determining Maturity Date and Computing Maturity Value

The maturity date is the due date of the note. The basic rules with respect to determining the maturity date are:

1. A specific date, such as "November 11th, 2006";

2. A specific number of months after the date of the note, such as "2 months after date";

3. A specific number of days after the date of the note, for example, "60 days after date".

When the life of the note is expressed in terms of days, it can be determined by:

- You need to count the days;
- Include the issue date and exclude the maturity date;
- Include the maturity date and exclude the issue date.

【Example 9.1】A note dated on October 3rd, and due in 60 days, would be due on _____.

Including the maturity date and excluding the issue date

Days left in October	28 days
Days in November	30 days
Days in December	2 days
Total	60 days
Maturity date	December 2nd

【Example 9.2】The note is issued on September 6th and the maturity date December 11th, determining the duration of the note.

Including the maturity date and excluding the issue date

Days left in September	24 days
Days in October	31 days
Days in November	30 days
Days in December	11 days
Total days	96 days

Interest is the cost of borrowing or of postponing payment. The maker of an interest-bearing note pays interest and reports interest expense, while the payee records interest earned, which is often reported as other gain on the income statement.

The interest rate is the rate charged for one year. Interest is calculated based on the following formula:

Maturity Value = Principal + Interest

Interest = Principal + Interest Rate + Time

【Example 9.3】 Interest on a $4000, 6%, 60-day is computed as :

$4000 × 6% × 60 / 360 = 40$

9.1.2 Accounting for Notes Receivable

【Example 9.4】 When merchandise was sold on account on April 1, 2006, terms 2/10, n/30. The entry to record this transaction would be:

Dr. Accounts receivable

Cr. Sales revenue

【Example 9.5】 On May 1, when a two-month, 6 percent note for $500 was received to replace its open account. The entry would be:

Dr. Notes receivable   500

Cr. Accounts receivable   500

【Example 9.6】 On July 1, the maturity date, when the note was paid, the entry would be:

Dr. Cash   505

Cr. Notes receivable   500

Interest income   5

9.1.3 Discounting Notes Receivable

Notes receivable are negotiable instruments, which means they can be sold to a bank or to other companies. This practice is known as **discounting**. When the bank "buys" the receivable, the bank is buying the right to collect the maturity value of the note at the maturity date.

The following key terms are used in accounting for discounted notes:

- Maturity date
- Maturity value—principal plus interest
- Discount period—the number of days between the date of sale to the bank and maturity date
- Bank discount—the amount deducted by the bank
- Proceeds of the discounted note—maturity value less bank discount

a.   Maturity Value = Face of Note + Interest Income

b.   Discount = Maturity Value × Discount Rate × Unexpired Time

c.   Net Proceeds = Maturity Value – Discount

【Example 9.7】 A company sold its note to Bank of China 30 days before its maturity at discounting rate of 10%, the note principal dated April 18, 2006, $ 4,000; maturity date June 30; interest rate, 8%.

Maturity value = $4,000 + ($4,000 × 8% × 73 ÷ 360) = $4,064.88

Discount = $4,064.88 \times 10\% \times 30 \div 360 = \$33.874$

Proceeds = $4,064.88 - \$33.874 = 4,031$

Dr. Cash   4,031

  Cr. Notes receivable   4,000

    Interest income   31

9.2　Accounts Receivable

Accounts receivable arise when a business sells goods and services on credit. Sales and profits can be increased by granting customers the privilege of making payment a month or more after the date of sale. However, no business wants to sell on credit to a customer who will be proved unable or unwilling to pay his or her account. Consequently, most business organizations have a credit department which investigates the credit worthiness of each prospective customer.

One of the key factors underlying the growth of the American economy is the trend toward selling goods and services on account. Accounts receivable comprise the largest financial assets of many merchandising companies.

Accounts receivable are relatively liquid assets, usually converting into cash within a period of 30 to 60 days. Therefore, accounts receivable from customers usually appear in the balance sheet immediately after cash and short-term in vestment and marketable securities. Assets that are relatively close to cash are referred to as current assets. Accounts receivable are a key factor in determining a firm's liquidity and may be discounted—used in raising a short-term bank loan, or sold to a factor. A Provision is usually made in the accounts of a firm to offset uncollectible accounts receivable (bad debts) as losses.

Sometimes companies sell merchandise on longer-term installment plans, requiring 12, 24, or even 48 months to collect the entire amount receivable from the customer. By definition, the normal period of time required to collect accounts receivable is part of a company's operating cycle. Therefore, accounts receivable arising from normal sales transactions usually are classified as current assets, even if the credit terms extend beyond one year.

Allowance Method of Accounting for Bad Debts

The allowance method estimates the total bad debts that are expected to result from the current period's sales, and records the expenses during the same period as the related sale. It's preferred because it matches collection losses with revenues in the period in which the sales were made. Also, the accounts receivable appear on the balance sheet at the amount of cash proceeds that are expected from their collection. For example, the company estimated that $1,000 of the accounts receivable will be uncollectible. Therefore, a debit of $1,000 is made to bad debt expense and a credit of $1,000 is made to allowance for doubtful accounts.

So the allowance method is required when bad debts are material in amount. Its essential features are:

Uncollectible accounts are estimated and the expense for the uncollectible accounts is matched against sales in the same accounting period in which the sales occurred.

Estimated uncollectible accounts are debited to bad debts expense and credited to allowance for doubtful accounts through an adjusting entry at the end of each period.

Actual uncollectible accounts are debited to allowance for doubtful accounts and credited to accounts receivable at the time a specific account is written off.

When there is a recovery of an account that has been written off as uncollectible, it is necessary to reverse the entry made when the account was written off, and to record the collection in the usual manner.

Recording Estimated Uncollectible Accounts

The allowance method estimates the total bad debts that are expected to result from the current period's sales, and records the expense during the same period as the related sale.

【Example 9.8】Assume that Brady Company has credit sales of $1,200,000 in 2006. $200,000 remains uncollected on December 31. The credit manager estimates that $12,000 of these sales will be uncollectible. The entry to record the estimated uncollectible is:

Dr. Bad debt expense　　　　　　　　　　　　12,000

　　Cr. Allowance for doubtful accounts　　　　　　　12,000

The accounts receivable appears on the balance sheet at the amount of each proceeds:

Brady Company

Balance Sheet

Accounts receivable　　　　　　　　　　　$200,000

Less: Allowance for doubtful accounts　　　　　12,000　　　$188,000

Write off a Bad Debt

With the allowance method, the bad debt expense is recorded in the year of sale. A contra asset account is used because an estimate is used and the specific accounts that will be uncollectible are not yet known.

When the specific account that is uncollectible is determined, the appropriate amount of the contra asset is transferred to its asset account. It therefore writes it off with a debit to the allowance for doubtful accounts, and a credit to a accounts receivable. Writing off an account against the allowance for doubtful accounts does not affect the total estimated realizable value of accounts receivable.

It is unlikely that the accounts written off during an accounting period will equal the allowance provided for bad debts. As a result, the allowance account may have a credit or debit balance prior to adjusting at the end of a year. A debit balance in the allowance would indicate that write-offs during the period were greater than what was allowed for; a credit balance would mean that write-offs were less than what was estimated to occur.

【Example 9.9】A Company authorizes a write-off the $500 balance owed by B Company on March 1, 2007. The entry to record the write-off is:

Dr. Allowance for doubtful accounts   500

    Cr. Accounts receivable   500

Bad Debt Recoveries

Generally, accounts are not written off until all avenues of collection have been exhausted. If a subsequent collection is made, the account is reinstated and the receipt is recorded.

【Example 9.10】B company unexpectedly paid the amount previously written off on July 31, 2007.

July 31

Dr. Accounts receivable   500

    Cr. Allowance for doubtful accounts   500

Dr. Cash   500

    Cr. Accounts receivable   500

9.3   Estimating the Amount of Bad Debt Expense

There are two general methods to estimate the required balance of the allowance for doubtful accounts.

9.3.1   Income Statement Method

The income statement method is based on historical data and future expectations. A percentage of credit sales is used to estimate the amount of bad debts.

This method emphasizes the matching of revenues and expenses; it estimates bad debt expense. The amount calculated is the amount of the entry and thus the amount of bad debt expense for the year.

【Example 9.11】On December 31, 2002, at the end of its annual accounting period, a company estimated its bad debts as half of 1% of its $1,790,000 of credit sales made during the year, and made an addition to its allowance for doubtful accounts equal to that amount. On February 3, 2003, management decided the $2,500 account of Big Co. was uncollectible and prepared an entry to write it off.

Dec. 31

Dr. Bad debt expense   8,950

    Cr. Allowance for doubtful accounts   8,950

0.5% × $1,790,000 = $8,950

Feb. 3

Dr. Allowance for doubtful accounts   2,500

    Cr. Accounts receivable   2,500

9.3.2　Balance Sheet Method

Rather than estimating a percentage of sales to be uncollectible, the balance sheet method is based on a percentage of total outstanding receivables estimated to become uncollectible. The balance sheet method focuses on the total estimated uncollectible receivable, which is the balance in allowance for doubtful accounts.

A sounder method of applying the balance sheet method is to prepare an aging schedule of individual customer accounts, which classifies outstanding accounts receivable in terms of how long each has been outstanding. The analysis is often called aging the accounts receivable. The aging of accounts receivable method applies a percentage to each class to estimate the amount of total receivables due that will not be collected. This method is more reliable because it draws attention to the specific accounts that are actually past due.

【Example 9.12】Sun company's analysis of accounts receivable based on past experience indicates that following had debt losses are likely to occur for each age group:

Age	Percent uncollectible
0-30 days	2%
31-60 days	4%
61-90 days	10%
Over 90 days	30%

On December 31, 2006, the following aged accounts receivable information is available:

Age of receivable	Amount receivable	Percent uncollectible	Allowance
0-30 days	$50,000	2%	$1,000
31-60 days	30,000	4%	1,200
61-90 days	5,000	10%	500
Over 90 days	3,000	30%	900
Total	$88,000		$3,600

Assume that the existing unadjusted balance in the allowance for doubtful accounts was $1,000 (credit).

December 31, 2016

Dr. Bad debt expense　　　　　　　　　　2,600

　　Cr. Allowance for doubtful accounts　　　　　2,600

To increase the allowance from $1,000 to $ 3,600.

Extracts from the balance sheet on December 31, 2016:

Current assets:

　　Accounts receivable　　　　　　　　$88,000

　　Less: allowance for doubtful accounts　　(3,600)　　$ 84,400

The previous example indicates that $88,000 is legally owed to the business, but the best estimate is that only $84,400 will be collected. Note that the focus of the balance sheet approach is not on the bad debt expense account but rather on the balance in the allowance for doubtful accounts.

Key Words and Phrases

discounting notes receivable	应收票据贴现
discount period	贴现期
maker	出票人
maturity date	到期日
maturity value	到期值
notes receivable	应收票据
payee	受票人
proceeds	贴现净值
promissory note	期票
aging of accounts receivable method	账龄分析法
allowance method	备抵法
bad debt recovery	坏账回收
bad debt expense	坏账费用
balance sheet method	资产负债表法
income statement method	利润表法
percentage of credit sales	赊销收入百分比法
write off	注销

Exercises

I. Fill in the blanks.

1. A _____ is a written promise to pay a specified amount of money either on demand or at a definite future date.

2. In published financial statements, notes receivable is often reported in the current assets section of the balance sheet after _____ and _____, but before inventory.

3. Parties to the note are the _____, who records a liability called notes payable, and the _____, who possesses an asset called notes receivable.

4. The _____ is the due of the note.

5. Notes receivable are negotiable instrument, which means they can be sold to a bank or to other companies. This practice is known as _____.

6. _____ is the number of days between the date of sale to the bank and maturity date.

7. The three major types of receivables are _____, notes receivable, and other receivables.

8. _____ are amounts owed by customers on account, resulting from the sale of goods and services.

9. When credit customers do not pay their debts, this _____ becomes an expense for the business.

10. The _____ method applies a percentage to each class to estimate the amount of total receivables due that will not be collected.

II. Computation.

1. Wiley purchased $7,000 of merchandise from Stamford Company on December 16, 2005. Stamford accepts Wiley's $7,000, 90-day, 12% note as payment. Stamford's annual accounting period ends on December 31 and it doesn't make reversing entries. Prepare entries for Stamford Company on December 16, 2005, and December 31, 2005.

2. Garden Company had a number of transactions involving receivables during the year 2005. Each of them is as follows.

Required: prepare journal entries to record these independent transactions on the books of Garden Company. Garden Company's year-end is December 31.

a. On November 15, 2005, Garden Company agreed to accept $500 in cash and a $2,000, 90-day, 8% note from Tiger Company to settle its $2,500 past-due account. Determine the maturity date and record the entry on November 15, December 31, and on the date of maturity.

b. Garden Company held a $1,800, 6%, 45-day note of Sunshine Company. At maturity, December 15, Sunshine dishonored the note. Record the dishonoring of the notes receivables.

3. On December 31, the end of its annual accounting period, a company estimated its bad debts as one half of 1% of its $650,000 of credit sales made during the year, and made an addition to its allowance for doubtful accounts equal to that amount. On the following April 10, management decided the $500 account of Sam Baker was uncollectible and wrote it off as a bad debt. Two months later, on June 9, Baker expectedly paid the amount previously written off. Give the general journal entries required to record these events.

Reading Materials

Accounts Receivable Turnover Ratio

Accounts receivable turnover is the number of times per year that a business collects its average accounts receivable. The ratio is intended to evaluate the ability of a company to efficiently issue credit to its customers and collect funds from them in a timely manner. A high turnover ratio indicates a combination of a conservative credit policy and an aggressive collections department, as well as a number of high-quality customers. A low turnover ratio represents an opportunity to collect excessively old accounts receivable that are unnecessarily tying up working capital. Low receivable turnover may be caused by a loose or nonexistent credit policy, an inadequate collections function, and/or a large proportion of customers having financial difficulties. It is also quite likely that a low turnover level indicates an excessive amount of bad debt.

It is useful to track accounts receivable turnover on a trend line in order to see if turnover is slowing down; if so, an increase in funding for the collections staff may be required, or at least a review of why turnover is worsening. To calculate receivables turnover, add together beginning and ending accounts receivable to arrive at the average accounts receivable for the measurement period, and divide into the net credit sales for the year. The formula is as follows:

$$\frac{\text{Net Annual Credit Sales}}{(\text{Beginning Accounts Receivable} + \text{Ending Accounts Receivable}) \div 2}$$

For example, the controller of ABC Company wants to determine the company's accounts receivable turnover for the past year. In the beginning of this period, the beginning accounts receivable balance was $316,000, and the ending balance was $384,000. Net credit sales for the last 12 months were $3,500,000. Based on this information, the controller calculates the accounts receivable turnover as:

$$\frac{\$3,500,000 \text{ Net credit sales}}{(\$316,000 \text{ Beginning receivables} + \$384,000 \text{ Ending receivables}) \div 2}$$

$$= \frac{\$3,500,000 \text{ Net credit sales}}{\$350,000 \text{ Average accounts receivable}}$$

$$= 10.0 \text{ Accounts receivable turnover}$$

Thus, ABC's accounts receivable turned over 10 times during the past year, which means that the average account receivable was collected in 36.5 days.

Here are a few cautionary items to consider when using the receivables turnover measurement:

- Some companies may use total sales in the numerator, rather than net credit sales. This can result in a misleading measurement if the proportion of cash sales is high, since the amount of turnover will appear to be higher than is really the case.

- A very high accounts receivable turnover number can indicate an excessively restrictive credit policy, where the credit manager is only allowing credit sales to the most credit-worthy customers, and letting competitors with looser credit policies take away other sales.

- The beginning and ending accounts receivable balances are for just two specific points in time during the measurement year, and the balances on those two dates may vary considerably from the average amount during the entire year. Therefore, it is acceptable to use a different method to arrive at the average accounts receivable balance, such as the average ending balance for all 12 months of the year.

- A low receivable turnover figure may not be the fault of the credit and collections staff at all. Instead, it is possible that errors made in other parts of the company are preventing payment. For example, if goods are faulty or the wrong goods are shipped, customers may refuse to pay the company. Thus, the blame for a poor measurement result may be spread through many parts of a business.

Quiz 5

1. Your business sells goods to a customer. There are two alternative terms on offer: 2,000 yuan on 60 days' credit or pay in full in cash on delivery(货到付款) and receive a discount of 5%. The customer takes the discount. How should the sale be recorded in the accounts?(　　).

  A. debit receivable 1,900 credit sales 1,900

  B. debit bank 1,900 debit discounts allowed 100 credit sales 2,000

  C. debit bank 1,900 credit sales 1,900

  D. debit bank 2,000 credit sales 1,900 credit discount allowed 100

2. On 1 May, your business sold goods to a customer for 1,000yuan on one month's credit, with the offer of a discount of 2% for payment within 7 days of the invoice date. On 4 May, the customer sent in payment by cheque, taking the early settlement discount offered. How should the payment be recorded in the accounts? (　　).

  A. debit bank 980 debit discounts allowed 20 credit receivables 1,000

  B. debit bank 980 credit receivables 980

  C. debit receivables 980 debit discount allowed 20 credit sales 1,000

  D. debit bank 1,000 credit discounts allowed 20 credit receivables 980

3. A business offers internet ordering and payment facilities. A customer purchases goods for 200yuan plus sales tax at 17.5% by credit card. How would this transaction be posted to the accounts of the buyer? (　　).

  A. debit bank 200 debit sales tax 35 credit Purchases 235

  B. debit. purchases 200 debit. sales tax 35 credit. Account payable 235

  C. debit. purchase 200 debit. sales tax 35 credit. Credit card account 235

  D. debit. account payable 235 Credit card account 235

4. Which of the following would be identified by matching a supplier statement against the transactions within the month? (　　).

  A. Incorrect calculations on invoices B. Non-delivery of goods charged

  C. Incorrect discounts   D. Duplication of invoice

5. Which of the following would be a good reason to maintain an aged creditor analysis? (　　).

  A. To detect potential bad debts

  B. To prevent the business missing opportunities to claim discount

  C. To provide a list of accounts payable outstanding

  D. To identify orders which have not been delivered

6. Which of the following would be a good reason to maintain an aged debtor analysis?

( ).

    A. To detect potential bad debts

    B. To prevent the business missing opportunities to claim discount

    C. To provide a list of accounts receivable outstanding

    D. To meet with the necessity of the debtor's.

7. A company is a supplier code number (2016). B purchased (purchases code 4000) goods costing 540 yuan plus 94.5 VAT (VAT code 1034) from A Company. How will this be posted to the computerized ledger of B company? ( ).

    A. debit purchase (4000) VAT (1034) Credit creditor (2016)

    B. debit 2016 debit. 4000 credit. 1034

    C. debit. 2016 credit. 4000   credit. 1034

    D. debit. 4000 credit. 1034 credit. 2016

8. Which of the following will not appear in the general ledger? ( ).

    A. Motor vehicles   B. Motor repairs   C. Discount received   D. Trade discounts

9. The double entry to record a discount received is ( ).

    A. debit. payables   credit discount received

    B. debit. discounts received   credit. accounts receivable

    C. debit discounts received   credit. accounts payable

    D. debit account receivable   credit. discount received

10. The double entry to record a discount allowed is ( ).

    A. debit. discount allowed   credit. receivable

    B. debit. discount received   credit. receivable

    C. debit. cash   credit. discount allowed

    D. debit. payable   credit. discount allowed

11. A business which is registered for VAT had a closing balance on its trade creditors account of 4,286yuan. During the period purchases on credit of 25,640 excluding VAT at 17.5% and payments to creditors totaled 29,660yuan. What was the balance at the start of the period on the trade creditors account? ( ).

    A. 266   B. 3,819   C. 4,753   D. 8,306

12. A business had accounts payable at the end of its accounting period of 6,538 and had made purchases during the period totaling 85,400yuan of which 46% were for cash. The balance on the accounts payable account at the start of the period had been 6711.

How much cash was paid to trade creditors during the period? ( ).

    A. 39,284   B. 39,457   C. 45,943   D. 46,289

13. The double entry for a purchase on credit would be ( ).

    A. debit purchases   credit. debtors

    B. debit stock   credit debtors

    C. debit creditors   credit purchases

    D. debit purchases   credit. creditors

14. If an invoice states that the settlement terms are 'net 30 days', this means that (   ).

A. the invoice amount, net of VAT, is payable 30 days from receipt of the invoice

B. the invoice amount, net of VAT, is payable 30 days from the invoice date

C. the invoice amount, gross of VAT, is payable 30 days from receipt of the invoice

D. the invoice amount, gross of VAT, is payable 30 days from the invoice date

15. The closing balance on the trade creditors account for a period was 3,528yuan. During the period cash paid to creditors was 11,583yuan. The opening balance on the trade creditors account was 2,660yuan. What were the credit purchases for the period? (   ).

    A. 10,715   B. 11,798   C. 12,451   D. 13,534

16. The following information is available about a business: (   ).

Opening creditors	14,550
Closing creditors	12,560
Payments for purchases in the period	85,460

Of the payments 35,640 were for cash purchases. What is the amount of purchases on credit for the period?

    A. 47,830   B. 48,810   C. 49,820   D. 83,470

17. Jack receives goods from Rose on credit terms and Jack subsequently pays by cheque. Jack then discovers that the goods are faulty and cancels the cheque before it is cashed by Rose.

How should Jack record the cancellation for the cheque in his books? (   ).

A. debit. creditors   credit. returns outwards

B. credit. bank   debit. creditors

C. debit. bank   credit. creditors

D. credit creditors   debit. returns outwards

18. To record goods returned inwards: (   ).

A. debit sales account and credit creditors account

B. debit returns inwards account and credit creditor's account

C. debit returns inwards account and credit debtor's account

D. debit debtors account and credit returns inwards account

19. The payment of cash to an account payable will (   ).

A. increase accounts receivable and reduce cash balance.

B. reduce cash balance and reduce current liabilities.

C. reduce accounts payable and increase purchases.

D. increase accounts payable and reduce cash balance.

20. Which one of the following is the correct posting from the purchase daybook? (   ).

A. debit. general ledger purchase account   credit. suppliers' accounts in purchase ledger

B. debit. general ledger purchase account   credit. cash

C. debit. suppliers' accounts in purchase ledger credit. general ledger purchase account

D. debit. cash   credit. general ledger purchase account

21. A trader who is not registered for sales tax purposes buys goods on credit. These goods have a list price of 2,000yuan and the trader is given a trade discount of 20%. The goods carry sales tax at 17.5%.

The correct ledger entries to record this purchase are to debit the purchases account and to credit the supplier's account with (　　).

      A. 1,600　　　　B. 1,880　　　　C. 2,000　　　　D. 2,350

22. We are registered for sales tax and purchased goods that had a net value of 700yuan on credit from X Company. What would be the debit to purchases if sales tax is payable at a rate of 17.5%? (　　).

      A. 577.5　　　　　　B. 700　　　　C. 822.5　　　　D. 848.48

23. Sales tax on a credit sale is recorded (　　).

      A. by the supplier when the invoice is issued and by the customer when the invoice is received

      B. by the supplier when the invoice is issued and by the customer when the invoice is paid

      C. by the supplier when the cash payment is received and by the customer when the invoice is received

      D. by the supplier when the cash payment is received and by the customer when the cash payment is made

Chapter 10　Fixed Assets and Depreciation

After studying this chapter, you should be able to:

- Explain the difference between capital and revenue;
- Identify the basic methods of valuing assets on current cost, fair value and value in use bases and their impact on profit measures and balance sheet values;
- Grasp the method for the depreciation for non-current asset, such as straight-line method, reducing balance method and revaluation method, and prepare accounts using each method and impairment;
- Prepare a non-current-asset register.

10.1　Overview

A non-current-asset is a resource acquired by an organization with the intention of using it to earn revenue for a long period of time such as land, buildings, motor vehicles, machinery and equipment. Non-current assets are economic resources that are owned for more than one year. They are possessed for business operations, not for direct sales. If they have physical form they are called tangible assets. If they do not have physical forms they are known as intangible assets, for example, patents, copyrights, licenses, goodwill, etc., though they have no physical form, intangible assets are also used in the business operations to yield revenue. Natural resources, such as oil wells, mineral deposits, gravel deposits, and timer tracts, are also long-term assets, but they can be physically consumed or used up. In accounting for long-term assets, we will first consider accounting for tangible assets, followed by intangible assets.

10.1.1　Major Categories of Fixed Assets

Plant and equipment items are often classified into the following groups:

1. Tangible Fixed Assets

The term "tangible" denotes physical substance, as exemplified by land, a building, or a machine. This category may be subdivided into two distinct classifications:

(1) Plant property subject to depreciation. Included are plant assets of limited useful life

such as buildings and office equipments.

(2) Land. The only plant asset not subject to depreciation is land, which has an unlimited term of existence.

2. Intangible Assets

The term "intangible assets" is used to describe assets that are used in the operation of the business but have no physical substance and are non-current. Examples include patents, copyrights, trademarks, franchises and goodwill. Current assets such as accounts receivable or prepaid rent are not included in the intangible classification, even accounts they are lacking in physical substance.

10.1.2 Long-term Assets

Long-term assets are the assets that have a useful life of more than one year, that are acquired for use in the operation of the business, and that are not intended for resale to customers. For many years, it is common to refer to long-term assets as fixed assets. But the use of this term fixed assets is declining because the word fixed implies that they last forever.

Assets not used in the normal course of business should not be included in this category. Thus land held for speculative reasons or buildings that are no longer used in the ordinary business operations should not be included in the property, plant and equipment category. Instead, they should be classified as long-term investments.

If an item is held for resale to customer, it should be classified as inventory—not plant or equipment—no matter how durable it is. For example, a printing press held for sale by a printing press manufacturer would be considered inventory, whereas the same printing press would be plant and equipment for a printing company that buys the press to use in its operations.

10.1.3 Capital Expenditures and Revenue Expenditures

Expenditures for the purchase or expansion of fixed assets are called expenditures and are recorded in asset accounts. Expenditures for ordinary repairs, maintenance, fuel and other items necessary to the ownership and use of plant and equipment are called revenue expenditures and are recorded by debiting expense accounts.

10.1.4 The Difference between Capital Expenditure and Revenue Expenditure

Capital expenditure is expenditure likely to increase the future earning capability of the organization, whereas revenue expenditure is associated with maintaining the organization's present earning capability.

10.1.5   The Nature of the Expenditure

Capital expenditure should be shown on the balance sheet. Revenue expenditure should be shown on the income statement.

Capital expenditure: the cost of acquisition of non-current assets, legal fees, carriage and delivery, and installation costs, test costs.

Revenue expenditure: the purchase or sale of inventories, wages, heat and light, the repair and maintenance of non-current assets.

10.2   Depreciation for the Fixed Assets

Many fixed assets have extended but limited lives. Since these assets help generate revenues throughout their useful lives, their costs must be reflected as expenses during that time. The cost of the non-current asset will contribute to the organization's ability to earn revenue for a number of accounting periods. It would be unfair if the whole cost were treated as an expense in the income statement in the year of acquisition, instead, the cost is spread over all of the accounting periods, in which the asset is expected to be making a contribution to earnings (this is known as the asset's useful life). The process by which this is achieved is called depreciation.

Depreciation is the process of allocating the cost of a fixed asset as expenses in the years when the asset helps generate revenue. Depreciation is an application of matching principle. Since land has an unlimited life, it is not depreciated. Chinese accounting standards permit the use, one of three commonly used methods. They are straight-line method, sum of the years' digits, and declining balance method. Methods differ in depreciation expense for each year, yet over the course of the entire life of the asset, total depreciation expense will be the same under all methods.

10.3   Accounting Entries for the Fixed Assets

(1) When obtaining an asset, it should be dealt with as follows.

Debit. Non-current asset / plant and machinery / or others

　　Credit. Cash or payables / creditors

It should be displayed on the balance sheet and should not be shown as an expense on the income statement because we have not yet begun to consume it in earning revenue.

(2) During the periods that the asset is in use, its useful life, we must allocate its original cost on some fair basis.

Debit. Depreciation charge (transferred into the income statement at the end of the period)

　　Credit. Accumulated depreciation (which is a contrary account of fixed asset)

The original cost of the fixed asset should be deducted to carrying amount which is shown on the balance sheet.

(3) Finally we reach a point where the whole of the original cost has been consumed and the carrying amount for the asset on the balance sheet has declined to zero (perhaps to some small residual value that it may realize on disposal).

Note:

The fair value of an asset refers to the estimated amount for which an asset could be sold. Depreciation is a way of allocating the cost of a non-current asset over a number of accounting periods.

10.4　Factors Affecting Depreciation

Four factors that influence depreciation are cost of the asset; estimated residual value (salvage value); estimated service life; and depreciation method.

The cost of the asset is determined by the cash or cash equivalent price paid to acquire the asset. There may be many cost components incurred to acquire and prepare the asset for its intended use.

The estimated residual value of the asset is an estimate of the net realizable value of the asset to an enterprise at the end of the asset's estimated service life. In determining the residual value of the asset, it is important to consider such costs as dismantling and disposal fees.

The estimated service life of the asset is the number of years that the asset is economically capable of performing its intended service.

10.5　Calculating Depreciation

Accounting for depreciation is the way to allocate the cost of an asset over its useful life span. Depreciation is a procedure to assign the cost of assets to expense for use of the asset. The idea of depreciation is simply a systematic write-off the original cost of an asset. The under-depreciated cost is called the book value which represents the remaining value. To calculate depreciation expense for an asset, such things as the original cost, estimated useful life and estimated salvage value must be made clear. The original cost is known when the asset is purchased but the estimated useful life and a salvage value is unknown at the time of purchase. It is known only on the basis of experience with similar assets.

10.5.1　Straight-line Method

The straight-line method allocates an equal amount of depreciation expense to each year in an asset's life. The method is based on the rationale that each year benefits equally from the asset's services.

【Example 10.1】

Assume that a machine has a cost of $4,000, an economic life of four years, and an estimated residual value of $500. Residual value is the amount the firm expects to receive from selling the asset at the end of its useful economic life. Annual straight-line depreciation expense is calculated by first subtracting the residual value from the cost. This difference is the depreciable basis. Then divide the depreciable basis by the number of years in the asset's estimated useful life.

The formula is as follows:

Depreciation Expenses per Annum = (Original Cost − Estimated Residual Value) ÷ Estimated Useful Life

For the machine, depreciation expense of each year is (4000-500)÷4=875. To record the depreciation expense, journal entry should be as follows:

Debit. Income statement or depreciation expenses   875

    Credit. Accumulated depreciation   875

When an asset is acquired in the middle of an accounting period, it is not necessary to compute depreciation expense to the nearest day or week since depreciation is based on an estimated useful life of many years, the depreciation applicable to any one year is only an approximation.

10.5.2 The Reducing-Balance Method

Accelerated methods of depreciation result in relatively large amounts of depreciation in the early years and smaller amounts in later years. It assumes that many kinds of plant assets are more efficient when they are new, so they provide more and better service in the early years of useful life. It is consistent with the matching rule to allocate more depreciation expense to the early years than to the later years if the benefits or services received in the early years are greater.

The accelerated methods also recognize that changing technologies make some equipments lose service value rapidly. As a result, it is realistic to allocate more to depreciation in current years than in future years. Another argument in favor of accelerated methods is that repair expense is likely to be greater in future years than in current years. Therefore, the total repair and depreciation expense remains fairly constant over a period of years. This result naturally assumes that the services received from the asset are roughly equal from year to year. The widely used accelerated depreciation methods are sum of the years' digits and declining balance method. In Chinese practice, only sum of the years' digits and declining balance method are accelerated methods that can be chosen.

1) Sum of the years' digits method

Under the sum of the years' digits method, the years in the service life of an asset are added. Their sum becomes the denominator of a series of fractions that are applied against the depreciable cost of the asset in allocating the total depreciation over the estimated useful life. The numerators of the fractions are the individual years in the estimated useful life of the asset in their reverse order. The formula of calculating depreciation using sum of the years' digits method is as follows.

(Cost – Estimated Residual Value) × Individual Year ÷ Sum of the Years' Digits

【Example 10.2】

According to this formula, we can calculate the first year's depreciation expense for the machine in our example: a machine's original cost of 3200 dollars, an economic life of five years, and an estimated residual value of 200 dollars.

Depreciation Schedule: Sum of the Years' Digits Method

Year	Original cost	Annual depreciation			Accumulated depreciation	Book value
		Sum of the years' digits fraction	Depreciation cost	Depreciation expense		
0	3200					3200
1		5 ÷ 15 × 3000=1000			1000	2200
2		4 ÷ 15 × 3000=800			1800	1400
3		3 ÷ 15 × 3000=600			2400	800
4		2 ÷ 15 × 3000=400			2800	400
5		1 ÷ 15 × 3000=200			3000	200

In the table above, the estimated useful life is five years. The sum of the years' digits is as follows: 1+2+3+4+5=15. From the schedule, note that the yearly depreciation is greatest in the first year and declines each year after that until it reaches the residual value.

2) Declining balance method

The declining balance method is an accelerated method of depreciation in which depreciation is computed by applying a fixed rate to carrying value of long lived asset. It is based on the same assumption as the sum of the years' digits method. Both methods result in higher depreciation charges during the early years of the life of the assets. The most common rate is a percentage equal to twice of the straight-line percentage, though any fixed rate might be used under the method. When twice the straight-line rate is used, the method is usually called the double declining balance method.

【Example 10.3】

In our earlier example, the machine had an estimated useful life of five years. Consequently, under the straight-line method, the percentage depreciation for each year was 20 percent.

Under the double declining balance method, the fixed percentage rate is 40 percentages. This fixed rate of 40 percent is applied to the remaining carrying value at the end of each year. Estimated residual value is not taken into account in computing depreciation except in the last two years of the useful life of the asset, when depreciation method is changed to the straight-line method. The depreciation schedule for this method is as follows.

Allocating the remaining book value over the remaining life by the straight-line method does not represent a change in depreciation methods. Rather, the switch to straight line is part of the declining balance method. This is the way in which we arrive at the desired residual value.

Annual Depreciation = Carrying Balance of the Fixed Asset × Rate of Depreciation

Depreciation Schedule: Double Declining Balance Method

Year	Original cost	Annual depreciation			Accumulated depreciation	Book value
		Sum of the years' digits fraction	Depreciation cost	Depreciation expense		
0	3200					3200
1		40% × 3200 = 1280			1280	1920
2		40% × 1920 = 768			2048	1152
3		40% × 1152 = 460.8			2508.8	691.2
4		(691.2 − 200) ÷ 2 = 245.6			2754.4	445.6
5		(691.2 − 200) ÷ 2 = 245.6			3000	200

Under this method, every year the expense is changing, greater in the earlier years than in the later years.

10.6 Controlling Tangible Non-Current Assets

First, we should understand that the means to obtain the control through computer and the carrier is non-current asset register. In the register, each asset would be given a code number whose function is to help to locate every particular asset.

For the controlling purpose, the information that might be contained in a non-current asset register is as follows:

(1) Management will need to be aware of:
- Whether any government grants have been obtained to assist in the purchase of the asset;
- The extent to which it is being used;
- The repairs that have been carried out on the asset and the cost of those repairs;
- The expiry dates of any licenses permitting the organization to use the asset.

(2) For accounting purposes, the following information is required:

Description of asset, date of purchase, name of supplier, cost of asset, asset code number, location, estimated useful life, estimated residual value, method of depreciation, depreciation amount to date, carrying amount, insurance details, and maintenance details, major amendments/refinements, disposal details.

The efficiency of the organization can be greatly improved if the register is stored on a computer.

10.7　Accounting for Intangibles

When acquiring intangible assets, their costs are capitalized in assets accounts at historical cost and expensed over their legal or useful life, whichever is shorter. The expense recognition process for intangible assets is called amortization. Straight-line amortization is usually used for intangible assets.

1. **Patents:** A patent is an exclusive right to sell or produce a commodity that has unique features. Issued by the federal government, a patent has a legal life of 17 years in the US. A patent may be developed in a company's own R&D lab or may be purchased from others. If the patent is purchased, its cost is simply the purchase price, and is recorded as Patent. The cost of the patent is amortized over the useful life of patent.

2. **Trade mark:** It is a name given by an organization to one of its products and which is used in the marketing of that product.

3. **Goodwill:** When a business is purchased, the negotiated price often exceeds the total fair market value of the individual assets minus the outstanding liabilities. This excess is called goodwill. Goodwill is an indication that the purchased business is worth more than its net assets, due to a good reputation, a strategic location, product superiority, or management skill.

Goodwill comprises business contacts, good stuff relations, and the right to occupy certain pieces of land, and so on.

(1)　When obtaining it, the entry is recordedas:

Debit. Goodwill or intangibles

　　Credit. Cash in Bank

(2)　When it occurs impairment, the entry is recorded as:

Debit. Impairment or income statement

　　Credit. Allowance for the impairment of non-current assets (contrary account to intangibles)

Note: Based on the prudent principle, we should estimate the current value of the assets to avoid overstating the value. If the current estimated value is less than the amount in the balance sheet, then the intangibles are said to be "impaired". Impairment occurs when the value of a non-current asset is less than its carrying amount in the balance sheet. In this situation, the goodwill is reduced to its new lower value and the difference is charged to the income statement as an expense.

Key Words and Phrases

cost method	成本法
equity method	权益法
subsequent expenditures	后续支出
the straight-line method	直线法
accelerated methods	加速折旧法
sum of the years' digits method	年数总合法
declining balance method	余额递减法
changes in estimate	估计变更
patents	专利
copyrights	版权
franchises	特许权
trademarks	商标权
goodwill	商誉
pre-operating expenses	开办费
deferred expenses	递延费用
revenue expenditure	收益性支出
capital expenditure	资本性支出
land improvements	土地改良
non-depreciable assets	非折旧资产
operating lease	经营性租赁
financing lease	融资性租赁
off-balance-sheet financing	表外融资
non-monetary exchange	非货币性交易
lump sum purchase	一揽子购入
construction in progress	在建工程
double declining balance method	双倍余额递减法
residual value	残值
carrying value	账面余额
fixed assets pending disposal	固定资产清理
depletion	折耗
production method	产量法
amortization	摊销
return on assets	资产报酬率
asset turnover	资产周转率

Exercises

I. Fill in the blanks.

1. _____ is the accounting process of allocating the periodic expiration of capital assets against the periodic revenue earned.

2. Four factors influence depreciation. They are cost of the asset, _____, _____and _____.

3. The _____ of the asset is the number of years that the asset is economically capable of performing its intended service.

4. The most common methods of depreciation are _____, _____, _____ and _____.

5. _____ is used if the asset provides equal benefits to a company throughout its useful life.

6. Two common methods for allocating depreciation on an accelerated basis are _____ and _____.

7. _____ ignores estimated salvage when computing depreciation.

8. The Total amount of depreciation expense is recorded in the contra asset account called_____.

9. _____ are assets which are used in the operation of the business but have no physical substance and are non-current.

10. The systematic allocation of the costs of these assets to the periods in which they provide benefits is called_____.

II. Computation.

1. Deluxe Ezra Company purchases equipment on January 1, Year 1, at the cost of $469,000. The asset is expected to have a service life of 12 years and a salvage value of $40,000.

Required:

(a) Compute the amount of depreciation for each of Years 1 through 3 using the straight-line depreciation method.

(b) Compute the amount of depreciation for each of Years 1 through 3 using the sum-of-the-years digits method.

(c) Compute the amount of depreciation for each of Years 1 through 3 using the double-declining balance method.

2. C Company installed a machine in its factory at a $114,000 cost. The machine's useful life was estimated at five years with a $5,700 trade-in value. Determine the machine's second-year depreciation with depreciation calculated in each of the following ways:

(a) Straight-line rate, (b) declining-balance basis at twice the straight-line rate, and (c) sum-of-the-years-digits basis.

Reading Materials

Fixed Assets

In contrast to current assets, long-term assets refer to those assets that will be realized or consumed within a period longer than one year of their acquisition, which are normally divided into fixed assets, intangible assets and deferred assets. Fixed assets refer to the assets whose useful life is over one year, unit value is above the prescribed criteria and where original physical form remains during the process of utilization, including building and structures machinery and equipment, transportation equipment, tools and implement, etc.

Fixed assets shall be accounted for at historical cost as obtained.

The cost of a plant asset is the purchase price, applicable taxes, purchase commissions, and all other amounts paid to acquire the asset and to ready it for its intended use.

Interest of loan and other related expenses for acquiring fixed assets, and the exchange difference from conversion of foreign currency loan, if incurred before the assets not having been put into operation or after been put into operation but before the final account for completed project is made shall be accounted as fixed assets value.

The measure of wearing out, consumption or other reduction in the useful life of a fixed asset whether arising form use, defluxion of time or obsolescence through technology and market changes is called depreciation.

The actual expenditures which incurred in the purpose of acquiring or technical reforming the fixed assets before available to the users, shall be shown separately as construction in progress in accounting statement.

In making an inventory of the fixed assets, the net profit or loss incurred in discard and disposal, and also overage, shortage of fixed assets shall be accounted as current profit and loss.

Part Three

Special Topics of Liability

Chapter 11 Payroll

After studying this chapter, you should be able to:

- Describe the documentation required for recording various elements of wages and salaries;
- Understand the duties of employers in relation to taxes, state benefit contributions and other deductions;
- Calculate gross wages for employees paid by hour, by output and salaried workers;
- Account for the wages;
- Recognize the need for payroll to be authorized and identify appropriate authorization security and control procedures;
- Understand wages and salaries represent a major element in the cost structure of most businesses.

11.1 Payroll Register

Wages and salaries represent a major element in the cost structure of most businesses. The precise nature of an enterprise's payroll records and procedures depends to a great extent on the size of its work force and the degree to which the recordkeeping is automated. In some form, however, two records are basic to most payroll systems: the payroll register and individual employee earnings records.

The payroll register is a detailed listing prepared each pay period of the company's complete payroll. Each employee's earnings and deductions for the period are contained in the payroll register. Table 11-1 illustrates a payroll register typical of those prepared by a firm with a small number of employees.

Note: FICA is referred to the federal insurance contributions act.

Payroll accounting procedures are influenced significantly by legislation enacted by the U.S. federal and state governments. These laws affect payroll accounting because they levy taxes based on payroll amounts.

(1) The federal insurance contributions act establishes the tax levied on both employee and employer. FICA tax applies to wages paid to employees during a calendar year, up to a certain amount per employee. Let us suppose that the tax was applied to the first $45,000 of an employee's wages and the tax rate is planned by legislation as 7.51%.

Table 11-1   Payroll Register

Week ended January, 2008

Employee	Total hours	Earnings		Gross wages	Deductions				Savings funds	Total inductions	Payment	
		Regular	Overtime		FICA tax	Feder- Income tax	Insurance				Net earnings	Check No.
Li Ying	42	320	24	344	25.83	43.3	3		2	74.13	269.87	
Chen Wei	40	180		180	13.52	15.6	2.5		1.5	33.12	146.88	

Total	----		96	1786	107.16	223.1	18.5		13.5	362.26	1423.7	

(2) Employers are required to withhold federal income taxes from wages and salaries paid to employee's. The amount of income tax withheld from each employee is based on the amount of the employee's wage or salary, the employee's marital status, and the number of withholding allowances to which the employee is entitled. Employers usually use wage-bracket tables prepared by the government to determine the amount of federal income taxes to withhold from each employee. Figures in our illustration are supposed to be based on such wage-bracket tables. The payroll register often serves as the basis for an entry to record the weekly payroll in the general journal. In our table, the entry would be:

Office salaries expense	724
Sales salaries expense	1062
FICA tax payable	107.16
Federal income tax withholding payable	223.10
Hospital insurance premiums payable	18.5
Savings bonds deductions payable	13.5
Payroll payable	1423.74

(3) Besides the FICA tax, which is levied on both employee and employer, the FUTA (Federal unemployment tax act) tax is levied only on the employer. Suppose that the law established the rate at 5.6% of the first $7,000 paid to each employee, but the employer is entitled to a credit against this tax for the state unemployment compensation taxes. The maximum credit allowed is 4.3% of the first $7,000 of each employee's wages. Hence, the effective FUTA rate on the employer will generally be 1.3% of the first $7,000 paid to each employee. The entry to record the employer's payroll tax liabilities for the week would be:

The various liabilities established in the entries recording the payroll and the employer's payroll taxes are settled by the employer making payments to the appropriate parties. The legislation levying various taxes also specifies the procedures for remitting these taxes to the government and establishes the reports an employer must file.

Payroll tax expense	$218.07
FICA tax payable 7.51%×$1786	$134.13
Federal unemployment tax payable 1.3%×$1786	$23.22
State unemployment tax payable 4.3%×$1786	$60.72

11.2   Individual Pay Slip

While a payroll register lists information on the gross earnings and deductions of all employees for each payroll period, the individual employee earnings records contain information on gross earnings and deductions for each employee for all payroll periods during the year. This record contains much of the information needed to permit the employer to comply with the various taxation and reporting requirements established by law. Its last column headed "Cumulative Gross Earnings" enables the employer to know when an employee's earnings for the year have exceeded the maximum amounts to which the FICA and unemployment taxes are applied.

Table   11-2

Employee's name	Fubo.Liu	Social security No.		5-16-32-4988		Employee No. 6	
Address	510, Yanfu street	Male		Single		Weekly pay rate	$320
	Daoli district	Female		Married		Hourly equivalent	$8
Date of birth	5.15,1976	Withholding allowances		3			
Postion	Clerk-analyst	Date of employment		June 1, 2000			
		Date employment ended					

续表

2010		Earnings			Deductions					Payment	
Period ended	Total hours	Regular	Over time	Gross	FICA tax	Federal income tax	Insurance	Savings funds	Total deductions	Net earnings	Check No.
Jan. 7	42	320	24	344	25.83	43.3	3	2	74.13	269.87	101
Jan.14	40	320		320	24.03	39.1	3	2	68.13	251.87	142
Jan. 21	44	320	48	368	27.64	48.1	3	2	80.74	287.26	186
Jan. 28	40	320		320	24.03	39.1	3	2	68.13	251.87	234
Feb.4	40	320		320	24.03	39.1	3	2	68.13	252.87	281
...											
Total											

11.2.1 Differences between Wages and Salaries

Wages: paid for a week;

Salaries: paid for a month.

11.2.2 Gross Pay, Deductions and Net Pay

1) Gross pay

The total amount earned in a week or month by an employee is called his or her gross pay.

2) Deductions

There are two sections which should be deducted from the gross pay which is shown in Figure 11-1.

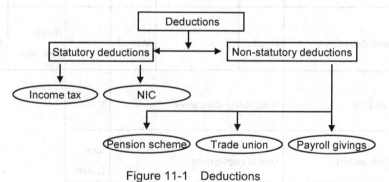

Figure 11-1 Deductions

11.2.3 Net Pay, Take-home Pay

Net pay is the residual pay that the gross pay deducts some deductions.

11.2.4   The Relationship between Gross Pay and Net Pay

The gross pay is deducted for the statutory deductions and non-statutory deductions and then the company will obtain the net pay or take-home pay. The relationship between gross pay and net pay is shown in Figure 11-2.

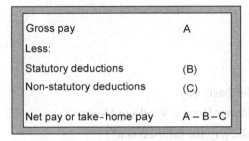

Gross pay	A
Less:	
Statutory deductions	(B)
Non-statutory deductions	(C)
Net pay or take-home pay	A – B – C

Figure 11-2   Relationship between Gross Pay and Net Pay

11.3   Procedure and Documentations

Now we will introduce the procedure and related documents.

11.3.1   Processing the Payroll

★ Calculate the gross pay for each employee for the period;

★ Calculate the income tax payable out of these earnings;

★ Calculate the NIC or state benefit contributions;

★ Calculate non-statutory contributions;

★ Prepare a pay slips showing gross pay, deductions, net pay;

★ Making payment to employee;

★ Payments to outsider agencies.

11.3.2   Documentations

The most important document is pay slip. In the pay slip there are many items such as gross pay, deductions and net pay, etc.

11.4   The Calculations for Pay

Gross Pay = Basic Pay + Other Pay (Overtime Pay + Shift Pay) + Bonuses and Commission Paid

11.4.1　Basic Pay

The first section: basic pay for hourly paid employee.

(1)　The source documentations relative to the working hours.

- Clock cards:
- Smart cards:
- Timesheets:
- Job cost record:
- Route card.

(2)　The calculations for basic pay.

Basic Pay = Wages Rate per Hour × Working Hours

The second section: basic pay for salaried staff.

There is a fix annual pay, then we can obtain the salary pay.

- Weekly paid 1 ÷ 52 the annual salary
- Fortnightly paid 2 ÷ 52 the annual salary
- 4 weekly paid 4 ÷ 52 the annual salary
- Monthly paid 1 ÷ 12 the annual salary

The third section: basic pay for employees paid by piecework.

Basic Pay = Number of Units Produced × Rate of Pay per Unit

Note: Sometimes the piecework system is backed up by a minimum wage. If a minimum wage is guaranteed, the basic pay will need to be increased to this level if the pay calculated using piecework rates is lower.

11.4.2　Supplementary Pay

Overtime: It must not be confused with flexitime. In a flexible system an employee is allowed to work extra hours earlier in the week or month, in return for which he will work fewer hours later on. His overall number of hour worked remains constant.

☆ Hourly paid workers

Hourly paid workers may be paid overtime at various different rates.

It may either be expressed as a higher monetary amount, or as a proportion of basic pay, such as 'time and a half', 'double time'.

☆ Weekly paid workers

☆ Salaried staff

Basic Rate per Hour = Annual Pay ÷ 52 ÷ Hours per Week

Hourly rate of overtime pay = Times of basic pay per hour × (Overtime hours − Deductions of hours)

Bonus: The essence of a bonus scheme is that additional pay will be earned if targets are achieved or exceeded. The scheme should set out the exact details and the dates of payment.

The bonus is based on some criteria which is shown in Figure 11-3.

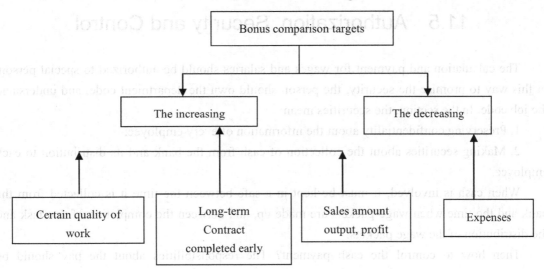

Figure 11-3 The Criteria for the Bonus

11.4.3 Commissions

It is based on the employee's performance and it is most commonly paid to sales men, based on the volume of sales that they have achieved in a given period.

Here shows an example of an individual employee's earning record:

Employee's name	Donald Bork	Social Security No.		719-23-4866		Employee No.		6
Address	510 Many lane	Male		Single		Weekly pay rate		320 dollars
	Archer, Fla. 32600	Female		Married		Hourly equivalent		8 dollars
Date of birth	MAY 5, 1977	Withholding allowance		3				
Position	Clerk-analyst	Date of employment		June, 2, 2000				
		Date employment ended						
2000	Total hours	Earnings			Deductions		Payment		Cumulative
Period ended		Regular	Over time	Gross	Income tax	Savings	Net earnings	Check NO.	gross earnings
January7	42	320	24	344	50	10	284	101	344
January14	40	320		320	10	10	300	142	670
January21	44	320	48	368	20	48	300	186	1032
January28	40	320		320	10	10	300	234	1532
---------	-------								

11.5   Authorization, Security and Control

The calculation and payment for wages and salaries should be authorized to special person. In this way to promise the security, the person should own the department code, and understand the job code. In the section, the securities mean:

1. Preserving confidentiality about the information of every employee;

2. Making securities about the collection of cash from the bank and its distribution to each employee.

When cash is involved, it must be kept in a safe between the time it is collected from the bank and the time when wage packets are made up, and between the completion of that task and the distribution of the wage packets.

Then how to control the cash payment? The responsibilities about the pay should be separated between payroll department and personnel department.

1)   The role of personnel department

Recruiting and engaging employees, the collecting about basic information relative to employee, basic work helpful to the calculation of wages and salaries (a personnel record card and a record of attendance card).

2)   The role of payroll department

The advantage or function of the control is as follows:

(1)   To ensure that employees who have left the organization are not still being paid.

(2)   To highlight whether dummy employees have been invented by employees in payroll as a way of committing fraud.

11.6   Accounting Treatment

Accounting treating is the core of accounting, if you can make accounting treatment independently, you will make further step.

11.6.1   Posting Payroll Details to the Main Ledger

The accounts relative to the wages are as follows:

- Expenses: wages and salaries expenses;
- Liabilities: wages and salaries control account;
- HM revenue and customers account—PAYE deductions, employees' NIC, employers' NIC;
- Pension payable account—employers', employees';
- Trade union payable account, other payable account;

● Assets: bank savings.

11.6.2 Accounting Entries

Dr. Wages and salaries expense account
    Cr. Wages and salaries control account

Dr. Wages and salaries control account
    Cr. HM revenue and customers account—NIC (employee's)
                                    —income tax

Pension creditor (employee's)

About employer is as follows:

Dr. Wages and salaries expenses
    Cr. HM revenue and customers account—NIC (employer's)
        Pension creditor (employer's)

Payment to the employee is as follows:

Dr. Wages and salaries control account
    Cr. Bank savings

【Example】

In a simple case of wages payable, let's assume that Hong Ying Corporation hired an employee with weekly payment of 1500yuan. Assume again that the end of the month, January 30th, the wages payable was 400yuan. Then accounting for the payroll would merely be like the following:

January 30

Dr. Salaried expense	400	
Cr. Salaries payable		400

February 2

Dr. Salaries expense	1100	
Salaries payable	400	
Cr. Cash		1500

Key Words and Phrases

gross pay	应付工资总额
net pay	实发工资
NIC (national insurance contributions)	国民保险税
PAYE (Pay as you earn)	预扣所得税

payroll	工资条
wages	周薪制
salaries	月薪制
highlight	使显著，使突出
dummy	挂名者，仿制样品，人体模型
invented	捏造的
committing fraud	实施诈骗犯罪
payroll accounting	工薪会计
pay period	工资支付期
federal	联邦的
withhold	预扣
marital status	婚姻状况
withholding allowance	预扣折让
wage-bracket table	工资税级表
hospital insurance premiums payable	应付住院保险费
savings bonds deductions payable	应付购买储蓄债券扣款
payroll payable	应付工资
payroll tax	应交税费
comply with	遵守
federal unemployment tax act	联邦失业税法
state unemployment compensation tax	州失业补贴税
federal unemployment tax payable	应付联邦失业税
cost structure	成本结构
overtime pay	加班工资
regular rate of pay	正常工资率

Exercises

I. Fill in the blanks.

1. The amount of federal income tax withheld from a person is based upon the individual _____ and _____.

2. From _____ will yield information pertaining to the number of exemptions an employee is filing.

3. The payroll _____ is the input for the payroll entry.

4. Generally, all payroll entries are recorded in the _____ journal.

5. The two types of payroll taxes imposed on the employer are _____ and _____.

6. The payroll tax expense entry is recorded in the _____ journal.

7. The tax that is paid by the employee and matched by the employer is _____.

II. Computation.

1. Complete the table below upon the employer's payroll obligations. Assume a state FUTA rate was 6.2% of the first $7,000 of each employee's wages and state rate of 5.4%

Employee	Amount earned This week	Accumulated Earnings	FUTA	SUTA
(a) I. Blanton	$200	$6,500	?	?
(b) P.Burday	250	5,500	?	?
(c) M.Fleming	275	7,500	?	?

2. Judy Bagon worked 44 hours during the first week in February of the current year. The pay rate is $3.5 per hour. Withheld from her wages were FICA 6.5 percent, federal income tax $21. Determine the necessary payroll entry.

Reading Materials

Efficiency

A newly issued report reveals in facts and figures what should have known in principle, that quite a lot of business companies are going to go under during the coming decade, as tariff walls are progressively dismantled. Labor and capital valued at $12billion are to be made idle through the impact of duty-free imports. As a result, 35, 000 workers will be displaced. Some will move to other jobs and other departments within the same firm. Around 15, 000 will have to leave the firm now employing them and work elsewhere.

The report is measuring exclusively the influence of free trade with Europe. The authors do not take into account the expected expansion of production over the coming years. On the other hand, they are not sure that even the export predictions they make will be achieved. For this presupposes that a suitable business climate lets the pressure to increase productivity materialize.

There are two reasons why this scenario may not happen. The first one is that industry on the whole is not taking the initiatives necessary to adapt fully to the new price situation it will be facing as time goes by. This is another way of saying that the manufacturers do not realize what lies ahead. The government is to blame for not making the position absolutely clear. It should be saying that in ten years' time tariffs on all industrial goods imported from Europe will be eliminated. There will be no adjustment assistance for manufactures who cannot adapt to this situation.

The second obstacle to adjustment is not stressed in the same way in the report; it is the attitude of the service sector. Not only are service industries unaware that the common market treaty concerns them too, they are artificially insulated from the physical pressure of international competition. The manufacturing sector has been forced to apply its nose to the grindstone for some time now, by the increasingly stringent import-liberalization program. The ancillary services on which the factories depend show a growing indifference to their work obligations. They seem unaware that overmanned ships, underutilized container equipment in the ports, and repeated work stoppages slow the country's attempts to narrow the trade gap. The remedy is to cut the fees charged by these services so as to reduce their earnings—in exactly the same way that earnings in industrial undertakings are reduced by the tariff reduction program embodied in the treaty with the European Community.

There is no point in dismissing 15, 000 industrial workers from their present jobs during the coming ten years if all the gain in productivity is wasted by costly harbor, transport, financial, administrative and other services. The free trade treaty is their concern as well. Surplus staff should be removed, if need be, from all workplaces, not just from the factories. Efficiency is everybody's business.

Chapter 12　Liability

After studying this chapter, you should be able to:

- Understand the definition and types of current liabilities;
- Explain notes payable and accounts payable;
- Comprehend the features of bonds payable;
- Understand the classification of bonds.

12.1　Current Liabilities

12.1.1　Definition and Types of Current Liabilities

A liability is debt borned by an enterprise, measurable by money value, which will be paid to creditor using assets, or services, which are generally classified into current liabilities and long-term liabilities. The FASB defines liability in its Statement of Financial Accounting Concept No.3 Elements of Financial Statements as "the probable future sacrifice of economic benefits arising from present obligations of a particular entity to transfer assets or provide services to other entities in the future as a result of past transactions or events." The Board states that an obligation must have three characteristics to be reported as a liability. (1)The obligation must involve a future sacrifice of cash, goods, of services; (2)It must be an obligation of the enterprise; and (3)The transaction or event giving rise to enterprise's obligation must already have occurred.

Current liabilities refer to the debts which should be paid off within a year or an operating cycle longer than a year, including short-term loans payable, notes payable, accounts payable, dividends payable etc.

In accordance with the degree of uncertainties, current liabilities can be further classified into definite liabilities, accrued liabilities, and contingent liabilities. Definite liabilities are debts whose amount to be paid, maturity date, and payee are clearly determinable. Definite liabilities include accounts payable, notes payable, salaries and wages payable, the current portion of long-term liabilities. Accrued liabilities arise from the recognition of expenses for which payment will be made in a future period. Contingent liabilities have an existence and an amount of liability that are uncertain and their incurrence depends on future contingencies.

12.1.2　Notes Payable

In most cases, the life of a note is somewhere between thirty days and one year, and the bank or loan company lends the borrowing company less cash than that is indicated on the face of the note. At the maturity date (when the loan is due), the borrowing company pays the lending institution the face amount of the note, and the difference between the face amount and the amount of the loan is treated as interest.

Notes payable are obligation in the form of written promissory notes. The maker of note promises to pay the face amount of the note on the due date. The due date is also called maturity date. It is issued whenever bank loans are obtained. Other transactions include the purchase of the real estate or costly equipment, the purchase of merchandise and the substitution of a note for a past-due account payable. Notes payable may be either interest-bearing or non-interest-bearing. And normally the interest rate is stated separately from the principle amount of the note.

【Example 12.1】

On October 1, 2009, F Company borrowed $ 400,000 from Commercial Bank and signed a three-month note with a face amount of $412,000. The journal entry to record this transaction is provided below.

October 1, 2009
Dr. Cash   400,000
    Discount on notes payable   12,000
        Cr. Notes payable   412,000

The "discount on notes payable" account serves as a contra account to notes payable on the balance sheet and represents interest that is not yet owed but will be recognized in the future. Assuming the financial statements are prepared monthly, one- third of the discount would be converted to interest expense each month by an adjusting entry of the following form.

Adjust for interest expense for the month:
Dr. Interest expense   4,000
    Cr. Discount on notes payables   4,000

For financial reporting purposes, the discount on notes payable is deducted from the notes payable account on the balance sheet.

Notes payable   412,000
Less: Discount on notes payable   4,000
Net of notes payable   408,000

【Example 12.2】

B Company could not pay its past-due $15,000 account to A Company. As an accommodation, on April 1, A company agreed to accept B Company's 3 months, 12%, $15,000 note in granting an extension on the due date of the debt.

B company recorded the issuance of the note as follows:
April 1
Dr. Accounts payable — A Company   15,000
    Cr. Notes payable   15,000

At each end of April, May and June, B Company recorded the following entry:

Dr. Interest expense 150

    Cr. Interest payable 150

Note that the note does not pay off the debt. Rather, the form of the debt is merely changed from an account payable to a note payable. A company should prefer holding the note to the account, because, in case of default, the note is a very good written evidence of the debt's existence and its amount.

When the note becomes due, B company will give A company a check for $450 and record the payment of the note and its interest with this entry:

On July 1, B company paid A Company the interest expense and principal.

Dr. Notes payable 15,000

    Interest expense 450

      Cr. Cash 15,450

If companies borrow funds from banks or other lenders by signing notes, it is financing activities in statement of cash flows.

In Example 12.2, assume that on April 1, A Company lent money to B Company and accepted B Company's 3 month, 12%, $15,000 note.

B Company recorded the issuance of the note as follows:

April 1

Dr. Cash 15,000

    Cr. Notes payable 15,000

12.1.3 Accounts Payable

Accounts payable are amounts that a company owed to others for goods, supplies, and services purchased on account. These extensions of credit are the practical result of a time lag between the receipt of the goods, supplies, or services and the corresponding payment. Accounts payable are usually recorded at an amount less any available cash discounts. If payment has not been made until after the discount period has lapsed, the additional amount paid is charged to an expense account entitled purchase discount lost.

Accounts payable are usually associated with inventory purchases. Most accounting systems are designed to record liabilities when the goods are received or, practically, when the invoices are received.

【Example 12.3】

If John's Company purchased office supplies from supplier on account invoice for total $20,000. The sum of the amounts was listed as a current liability on John's Company balance sheet. The journal entry is as follows:

Dr. Office supplies 20,000

    Cr. Accounts payable 20,000

When John's Company paid the bill, John's Company should record as follows:

Dr. Accounts payable   20,000

     Cr. Cash   20,000

The size of the balance in accounts payable can be an important indicator of a company's financial condition, especially in the retail industry where suppliers are heavily relied upon to provide merchandise.

12.2   Long-term Liabilities

Long-term liability refers to the debts which will be redeemed after a year or an operating cycle longer than a year, including bonds payable, long-term accounts payable, etc. Because bonds are a common form of long-term debt, they will be used to explain the key accounting procedures for long-term liabilities.

12.2.1   The Fundamental Concepts

1)   Definition of Bonds

A bond is certificate promising to pay its holder a specified sum of money plus interest at a stated rate. When a corporation issues bonds, it usually incurs two distinct obligations: (1) to pay the face amount of the bonds at a specified maturity date, and (2) to pay periodic interest at a specified percentage of the face amount.

2)   Features of Bonds

If you purchase a bond, you will receive a bond certificate. This certificate spells out the terms of agreement between the issuer and the investor. These terms include the denomination of bond, maturity date, the stated rate of interest, the interest payment terms, and any other agreements made between the borrower and investor.

3)   Denomination of Bond

Most bonds have a denomination of $1,000 although in recent years $5,000 and $10,000 bonds have become common. The denomination of a bond is often referred to as face value or maturity value. It is always on this amount that the required interest payment is calculated. A total bond issue usually contains hundreds of thousands of individual bonds. For example, a $10 million bond issue may be made up of 10,000 individual $1,000 bonds. After bonds are issued, they are traded daily on organized securities exchanges. This enables investors to sell and purchase bonds freely.

4)   Maturity Date

The date that the principal of bond is paid is called the maturity date. Bonds usually mature in from 5 years to more than 30 years from their date of issue.

5)   Stated Interest Rate and Interest Payment Dates

The stated interest rate of bond is often referred to as nominal interest rate and is specified on the bond at the time it is issued. This rate does not change over the life of the bond. Most bonds pay interest semiannually, however, the stated interest rate is an annual rate based on the face value of the bond. For example, a $1000, 10% bond that pays interest on January 1 and July 1 will pay interest of $50 ($1000×10%×6÷12) on each of these dates until it matures.

6)　Other agreements

Bondholders are unable to vote for corporate management or participate in corporate affairs in the way that stockholders do. Therefore, bondholders often insist on written items as part of the bonds agreement. They usually include restrictions as to dividends, working capital and the issuance of additional long-term debt. The purpose of these agreements is to encourage that the borrower will maintain a strong financial position to meet the interest and principal payments.

12.2.2　Types of Bonds

There are several different types of bonds, including term, serial, coupon, registered, secured, unsecured, convertible and callable bonds.

1)　Term Bonds and Serial Bonds

When all bonds of an issue mature at the same time, they are called term bonds. If the maturities are spread over several dates, they are called serial bonds.

2)　Coupon Bonds and Registered Bonds

Coupon bonds are not registered in the name of individual holders but are negotiable by whoever holds them. In order to receive interest payment, the current holders simply clip off a coupon and redeem it at an authorized bank. Coupon bonds don't offer much safety to the holder. If the investor loses the coupon, he or she will not receive interest. Registered bonds may be transferred from one owner to another only by endorsement on the bond certificate, and the issuing corporation must maintain a record of the name and the address of each bondholder. Interest payments are made by check to the owner of record.

3)　Secured Bonds and Unsecured Bonds

An unsecured bond is called a debenture. A debenture bond issued by a very large and strong corporation may have a higher investment rating than a secured bond issued by a corporation in less satisfactory financial condition. Some bonds are secured by the borrower's collateral or specified assets. These secured bonds are often referred to as mortgage bonds.

4)　Convertible Bonds

A convertible bond may be exchanged at the potion of the bondholder for a specified number of shares of common stock. Convertible bonds are usually callable, which means that the borrower, or issuer, is able to call the bonds prior to their maturity.

5)　Callable Bonds

Almost all bonds are callable, which means that the corporation has the right to redeem the bonds in advance of the maturity date by paying a specified call price. To compensate bondholders for being forced to give up their investments, the call price usually is somewhat higher than the face value of the bonds.

12.2.3　Accounting for Bonds Payable

Accounting for bonds payable closely parallels accounting for notes payable. The accountable events for a bond issue usually are (1) issuance of the bonds, (2) semiannual interest payments, (3) accrual of interest payable at the end of each accounting period, and (4) retirement of the bonds at maturity.

(1) Issuance at Par.

【Example 12.4】

Mars Company issues bonds on January 1, 2001, with a principal amount of $100 million to be repaid in 10 years and a 12% coupon rate of interest payable semiannually, the market interest rate is 12%.

Mars should make the following payments:

Principal: $ 100 million, due in 10 years

Interest: $ 6 million, due at the end of each six-month period, for 10 years

$100M×12%×1/2 = $6M

Because the market rate and the coupon rate of interest are the same, the bonds sell at their face value of $100 million. The quoted annual interest rate of 12% is actually 6% each six-month period since the bonds pay interest each six months.

The following entry would be recorded in the bookkeeping. On January 1, 2001.

Cash　　　　　　　　　　　　　　　100,000,000

　　Bonds payable　　　　　　　　　　　　　　100,000,000

Each six months for 10 years, Mars Company should recognize interest expense and pays $6 million to the bondholders each June 30 and December 31 from 2001 through 2010.

　　Interest expense　　　　　　　　　　　6,000,000

　　　　Cash (interest payable)　　　　　　　　　　6,000,000

On the maturity date, December 31, 2010, Mars Company pays $100 million in bond principal and retires the bonds payable.

Bonds payable　　　　　　　　　100,000,000

　　Cash　　　　　　　　　　　　　　　100,000,000

Interest expense　　　　　　　　　6,000,000

　　Cash (interest payable)　　　　　　　　6,000,000

(2) Issuance between Interest Rates.

The semiannual interest rates (such as January 1 and July 1, or April 1 and October 1) are printed on the bond certificates. However, bonds are often issued between the specified interest rates. The investor is then required to pay the interest accrued to the date of issuance in addition to the stated price of the bond. This practice enables the corporation to pay a full six months' interest on all bonds outstanding at the semiannual interest payment date. The accrued interest collected from investors who purchase bonds between interest payment dates is thus returned to them on the next interest payment date.

Assume that A Corporation issues $1 million of 12% bonds at a price of $ 100 on May 1 — two months after the date printed on the bonds. The amount received from the bond purchasers now will include two months' accrued interest, as follows:

Cash	1,020,000	
Bonds payable		1,000,000
Bonds interest payable		20,000

Issued $1,000,000 face value of 12% year bonds at 100 plus accrued interest for two months ($1,000,000×12%×2/12 = $20,000).

Four months later on the regular semiannual interest payment date, a full six months' interest ($60 per $1000 bond) will be paid to all bondholders, regardless of when they purchased their bonds. The entry for the semiannual interest payment is illustrated below:

Bonds interest payable	20,000	
Bonds interest expense	40,000	
Cash		60,000

Paid semiannual interest on $1,000,000 face value of 12% bonds.

Now consider these interest transactions from the standpoint of the investors. They paid for two months' accrued interest at the time of purchasing the bonds and then received checks for six months' interest after holding the bonds for only four months. They have, therefore, been reimbursed properly for the use of their money for four months.

When bonds are subsequently sold by one investor to another, they sell at the quoted market price plus accrued interest since the last interest payment date. This practice enables the issuing corporation to pay all the interest for an interest period to the investor owning the bond at the interest date. Otherwise, the corporation would have to make partial payments to every investor who bought or sold the bond during the interest period.

(3) Issuance at a Discount or a Premium.

Bonds are usually issued at their face value, at a premium or at a discount depending on whether the nominal interest rate on the bonds is equal to, more than or less than, respectively, the applicable current market rate of interest. When the market rate is greater than the nominal interest rate, a bond will be issued at a discount and vice versa. Thus, a bond premium or a discount should be considered as an adjustment to interest expense over the life of the bond.

Assume that on January 1, 1997, B Corporation issued one hundred $1000, 10% bonds that mature in 10 years at 97% of their face value. Interest is paid on June 30 and December 31. The entry to record the issue of the bonds would be:

Jan.1, 1997

Cash	97,000	
Discount on bonds payable	3,000	
Bonds payable		100,000

On June 30, the entry to record the first semiannual interest payment is:

June 30, 1997

Dr. Bond interest expense   5,000 ($100,000×10%×6/12 = $5,000)

    Cr.Cash   5,000

The journal entry to record the semiannual amortization of bond discount under straight-line method would be:

Jan. 30, 1997

Dr. Bond interest expense   150 ($3,000×10%×6/12=$150)

    Cr. Discount on bonds payable   150

The journal entry to record the amortization of discount on bonds will be made at each interest payment date over the life of the bonds.

On December 31, 2006, the journal entry to record the payment of principal of bonds, last semiannual interest and last amortization of discount on bonds would be:

Dec. 31, 2006

Dr. Bonds payable   100,000

    Bonds interest expense   5,000

        Cr. Cash   105,000

Dr. Bonds interest expense   150

    Cr. Discount on bonds payable   150

An alternative method for the amortization of bond discount or premium is known as the effective interest method, which reflects a constant rate of interest over the life of the bonds. However, it is much more complex than the straight-line method.

Key Words and Phrases

amortize	摊销
accounts payable	应付账款
accrued liability	应计负债
bond discount	债券折价
bond premium	债券溢价
bondholder	债券持有人
bonds payable	应付债券
bond certificate	债券证明书
callable bonds	可赎回债券
convertible bonds	可转换债券
current liability	应付负债
face value	面值
long-term liabilities	长期负债

maturity date	到期日
nominal interest rate	名义利率
notes payable	应付票据
registered bonds	记名债券
serial bonds	分期还本债券
straight-line method	直线法
secured bonds	抵押债券
term bonds	一次还本债券

Exercises

I. Fill in the blanks.

1. _____ is a certificate promising to pay its holder a specified sum of money plus interest at a stated rate.

2. _____ is a contract through which corporation of issuing bonds enters with the bondholders.

3. _____ means the principal of each bond, generally $1,000 per bond.

4. All bonds of an issue mature at the same time are called _____.

5. The bonds maturities are spread over several dates, they are called _____.

6. The bond may be exchanged for other securities under certain conditions are called _____.

7. _____ issued by a corporation that reserves the right to redeem bonds before maturity.

8. _____ are issued by corporation.

9. _____ sometimes referred to as government bonds, which are issued by the federal government.

II. Choose the best answer for each of the following statements.

1. Typical liability accounts include _____.
   A. accounts payable, bank loan, wages payable, drawings
   B. accounts payable, bank overdraft, wages payable, stationery
   C. accounts receivable, bank overdraft, wages payable, unearned revenue
   D. accounts payable, borrowing from the public, bank overdraft, wages payable

2. Tiger Company borrowed $20,000 from its bank for a period of six months at an annual interest rate of 12%, all due at maturity date. The interest on this loan is stated separately. Which of the following is recorded at the date of borrowing? _____.
   A. Notes payable   B. Interest payable
   C. Prepaid Interest   D. Interest expense

3. Stewart Corporation sells exercise equipment carrying a three-year warranty. The liability for repairs on the equipment should be recognized_____.

    A. evenly over the three-year warranty period

    B. three years after the equipment is sold when the warranty expires

    C. in the accounting period when customers bring equipment in for repairs

    D. in the accounting period when the exercise equipment is sold

III. Computation.

Selected transactions for the H Company are given below. H's annual accounting period ends on September 30.

On June 1, 2012, purchased merchandise from the Green Company for $198,000, terms 1/10, n/30.

June 11, gave the Green Company a $198,000, 10%, 180-day note in payment of the open account.

June 12, borrowed $300,000 from the Western Trust Company and gave Western a one year, 9%, note for $300,000.

Required:

a. Prepare journal entries to record the transactions on June 1, 11 and 12;

b. Prepare necessary adjusting entries on September 30;

c. Show the presentation of the liabilities in the September 30, 2012, balance sheet;

d. Prepare journal entries to record payment of the Green note on December 7, 2012 and the Western note on June 12, 2013.

Reading Materials

Difference between Provision and Contingent Liability

Both provisions and contingent liabilities and also contingent assets are governed by "IAS 37: Provisions, Contingent Liabilities and Contingent Assets". The objective of creating provisions and contingent liabilities is in line with prudence concept in accounting where assets and liabilities should be matched against incomes and expenses for a given financial year. This practice is done to ensure that the year-end financial statements are presented in a realistic manner where assets are not overvalued and liabilities are not undervalued. The key difference between a provision and a contingent liability is that provision is accounted for at present as a result of a past event whereas a contingent liability is recorded at present to account for a possible future outflow of funds.

What is a Provision?

A provision is a decrease in asset value and should be recognized when a present obligation arises due to a past event. The timing is as to when the said obligation arises and the amount is often uncertain. Commonly recorded provisions are, provision for bad debts (debts that cannot be recovered due to insolvency of the debtors) and provision for doubtful debts (debts that are unlikely to be collected due to possible disputes with debtors, issues with payments days etc.) where the organization makes an allowance for the inability to collect funds from their debtors due to nonpayment. Provisions are reviewed at the financial year end to recognize the movements from the last financial year's provision amount and the over provision or under provision will be charged to the income statement. The usual provision amount for a provision will be decided based on company policy. For example, a company may have a policy is to make an allowance of 4% of debtors for bad and doubtful debts. In that case, if the total debtors amount to $ 10,000 the allowance will be $400.

What is a Contingent Liability?

For a contingent liability to be recognized there should be a reasonable estimate of a probable future cash outflow based on a future event. For instance, if there is a pending lawsuit against the organization, a possible cash payment may have to be made in the future in case the organization loses the lawsuit. Either winning or losing the lawsuit is not known at present thus the occurrence of the payment is not guaranteed. The recording of the contingent liability depends on the probability of the occurrence of the event that gives rise to such liability. If a reasonable estimate cannot be made regarding the amount, the contingent liability may not be recorded in the financial statements.

What is the difference between Provision and Contingent Liability?

Provision vs Contingent Liability	
Provision is accounted for at present as a result of a past event.	Contingent liability is recorded at present to account for a possible future outflow of funds.
Occurrence	
The occurrence of provisions is certain.	The occurrence of contingent liability is conditional.
Estimate	
The amount of provision is largely not certain.	A reasonable estimate can be made for the amount of payment.
Inclusion in Statement of Financial Position	
Provision is recorded as a decrease in assets in statement of financial position.	Contingent liability is recorded as an increase in liabilities in statement of financial position.
Inclusion in Income Statement	
Increase or decrease of provisions is recorded in the income statement.	Contingent liability is not recorded in the income statement.

Part Four

Special Topics of
Owners' Equity

Chapter 13 Owners' Equity—Partnership Accounting

After studying this chapter, you should be able to:

- List characteristics of partnerships.
- Explain advantages and disadvantages of partnerships.
- Understand allocating net income among the partners.
- Journalize the entries for dividing partnerships net income and loss.
- Journalize the entries for admission of a new partner.
- Journalize the entries for liquidating partnership.

A business can be organized in one of the three major forms—sole proprietorship, partnership, or corporation. A sole proprietorship is a separate organization with a single power. A partnership is a voluntary organization that is created by a partnership contract and joins two or more individuals together as co-owners.

13.1 Characteristics of Partnerships

Articles of Partnership: Good business practice calls for a written agreement among the partners, which contains provisions on the formation of the partnership, capital contributions of each partner, profit and loss distribution, admission and withdrawal of partners, withdrawal of funds, and dissolution of the business.

Unlimited Liability: Each partner in a general partnership is individually liable for the obligation of the firm regardless of the amount of personal investment.

Limited Life: Many events may cause the dissolution of a partnership. These include the expiration of the agreed-on term of partnership; the accomplishment of the business objective; the admission of a new partner; the withdrawal, the death, or bankruptcy of an existing partner; and the issuance of court.

Co-ownership of Property: Assets contributed by partners become partnership property jointly owned by all partners. Unless there is a contract to the contrary, each partner has an equal right to possess firm property for partnership purposes.

Participation in Profits and Losses: Profits and losses are distributed among the partners according to the partnership agreement. If no agreement exists, profits and losses must be shared equally.

13.1.1　Advantages and Disadvantages of Partnerships

The partnership form of business organization is less widely used than sole proprietorship and corporate forms. For many business purposes, however, the advantages of the partnership form are greater than its disadvantages.

A partnership is relatively easy and inexpensive to organize, requiring only an agreement between two or more persons. A partnership has the advantage of bringing together more capital, managerial skills, and experiences than doing a sole proprietorship. Since a partnership is a non-taxable entity, the combined income taxes paid by the individual partners may be lower than the income taxes that would be paid by a corporation, which is a taxable entity.

A major disadvantage of the partnership form of business organization is the unlimited liability feature for partners. Other disadvantages of a partnership are that its life is limited, and one partner can bind the partnership to contracts. Also, raising large amounts of capital is more difficult for a partnership than for a corporation.

13.1.2　Allocating Net Income among the Partners

A special feature of a partnership is the need to allocate the firm's net income among its partners. Allocating partnership net income means computing each partner's share of total net income (or loss) and crediting this amount to the partner's capital account. The amount that an individual partner withdraws during the year may differ substantially from the amount of partnership net income allocated to that partner. All partners pay personal income taxes on the amount of partnership income allocated to them.

Partners have great freedom in deciding how to allocate the firm's net income among themselves. In the absence of prior contract, state laws generally provide for an equal split among the partners. But this seldom happens. Partners usually agree well in advance how the firm's net income will be allocated.

In following paragraphs, we illustrate partnership agreements that recognize these differences.

1. Fixed or Capital Basis

Profits and losses are generally divided equally, in a fixed ratio, or in a ratio based upon the amounts of capital contributed by the partners.

【Example 13.1】The partnership agreement of Stone and Mills is to share on an equal basis, Stone and Mills have capital balances of $60,000 and $40,000 respectively. The net income for the first year of operation was $75,000. The journal entry for the allocation of the net income will be:

Income summary	75,000	
Stone, capital		37,500
Mills, capital		37,500

If, however, capital investment is to be the determining factor, the entry will run as follows:

Income summary	75,000	
Stone, capital		45,000
Mills, capital		30,000

2. Salary Basis

One method of recognizing differences in partners' abilities and amount of time devoted to the business is to provide salary allowances to partners. Since partners are legally not employees of the partnership, such allowances are treated as divisions of the net income and are credited to the partners' capital accounts.

【Example 13.2】 The partnership agreement of Stone and Mills provides for monthly salary allowances. Stone is to receive a monthly allowance of $2,500, and Mills is to receive $2,000 a month. Any net income remaining, after the salary allowances are to be divided equally. Assume also that the net income for the year is $75,000.

	Stone	Mills	Total
Salary allowance	$30,000	$24,000	$54,000
Remaining income	10,500	10,500	21,000
Net income	$40,500	$34,500	$75,000

The entry for dividing net income is as follows:

Income Summary	75,000	
Stone, Capital		40,500
Mills, Capital		34,500

【Example 13.3】 Assume the same salary and interest allowances as in the above example, but the net income is $50,000. The salary and interest allowances total $37,200 for Stone and $28,800 for Mills. The sum of these amounts, $66,000, exceeds the net income of $50,000 by $16,000. It is necessary to divide the $16,000 excess between Stone and Mills. Under the partnership agreement, any net income or net loss remaining after deducting the allowances is divided equally between Stone and Mills. Thus, each partner is allocated one-half of the $16,000, and $8,000 is deducted from each partner's share of the allowances. The final division of net income between Stone and Mills is shown below.

Net income		$50,000

Division of net income:

	Stone	Mill	Total
Salary allowance	$30,000	$24,000	$54,000
Interest allowance	7,200	4,800	12,000
Total	$37,200	28,800	66,000
Remaining loss	-8,000	-8,000	-16,000
Net income	$29,200	$20,800	$50,000

For the above example, the entry to close the income summary account is shown below.

Income summary	50,000	
Stone, capital		29,200
Mills, capital		20,800

13.2　Admission of a New Partner

An individual may gain admission to become partnership in either of two ways: (1) by buying an equity interest from of one or more of the present partners, or (2) by making an investment in the partnership. When an incoming partner purchases an equity interest from a present member of the firm, the payment goes personally to the old partner, and there is no change in the assets or liabilities of the partnership. On the other hand, if the incoming partner acquires an equity interest by making an interest via making an investment in the partnership, the assets of the firm are increased by the amount paid in by the new partner.

13.2.1　By Purchase of an Interest

When a new partner buys an equity interest from a present member of a partnership, the only change in the account will be a transfer from the capital account of the selling partner to the capital account of the incoming partner.

Assume, for example, that Tony has $80,000 equity interest in the partnership of Tony, David and Steven. Partner Tony arranges to sell her entire interest to Allen for $120,000 cash, partner David and Steven agree to admission of Allen, and the transition is recorded in the partnership accounts by the following entry.

Tony, capital	80,000	
Allen, capital		80,000

Note that the entry in the partnership accounts is for $80,000, the balance of Tony's capital balance. The entry does not indicate the price paid by Allen to retiring partner. The payment of $120,000 by Allen to Tony was a personal transaction between these two individuals; it does not affect the assets or liabilities of the partnership and, therefore is not entered in the partnership accounting records.

13.2.2　By Investing in the Firm

When a new partner acquires his or her equity by making an investment directly into the firm, the investment therefore increases the partnership assets and also the total owners' equity of the firm.

Assume that X and Y are partners, each has a capital account of the $100,000. They agree to admit Z to a one-half interest in the business upon his investment of $200,000 in cash. The entry to record the admission of Z would be as follows:

Cash		200,000	
	Z, capital		200,000

Although Z has a one-half equity in the net assets of the new firm of X, Y, Z, he is not necessarily entitled to receive one-half of profits. Profits sharing is a matter for agreement among the partners; if the new partnership contract contains no mention of profit sharing, the assumption is that the three partners intended to share profits and losses equally.

13.3 Liquidation of a Partnership

A partnership is terminated or dissolved whenever a new partner is added or an old partner withdraws. However, the termination or dissolution of the partnership does not necessarily indicate that the business is to be discontinued, often the business continues with scarcely any outward evidence of the change in membership of the firm, which may or may not be followed by liquidation.

The process of dissolving a partnership is referred to as liquidation. Liquidation of a partnership spells an end to the business. The three steps typically taken in an orderly liquidation are (1) the sale of the business; (2) division of the gain or loss from the sale of the business; (3) distribution of cash.

13.3.1 Sale of the Business

The partnership of A, B and C sells its business to the North Corporation. The balance sheet appears as follows:

【Example 13.4】

Balance Sheet

December 31, 2016

Cash	$60,000		Accounts payable	$10,000
Inventory	100,000		A, capital	140,000
Other assets	150,000		B, capital	120,000
			C, capital	40,000
Total	$310,000		Total	$310,000

The terms of the sale provide that the inventory and other assets will be sold to the North of corporation for a consideration of $160,000. The liabilities will not be transferred to North corporation, but will be paid by the partnership out of existing cash plus the proceeds of the sale, prior to any distribution of cash to the partners. The entry to record the sale of the inventory and other assets to North Corporation is:

Cash	160,000
Loss on sale of business	90,000

| Inventory | 100,000 |
| Other assets | 150,000 |

13.3.2 Division of the Gain or Loss from Sale of the Business

The gain or loss from the sale of the business must be divided among the partners at the agreed profit-and-loss sharing ratio before any cash is distributed to them. The amount of cash to which each partner is entitled in liquidation cannot be determined until each capital account has been increased or decreased by the proper share of the gain or loss on disposal of the assets. Assuming that A,B,C share profits and losses equally, the entry to allocate the $90,000 loss on the business as follows:

A, capital	30,000	
B, capital	30,000	
C, capital	30,000	
Loss on sale of Business		90,000

13.3.3 Distribution of Cash

The balance sheet of A, B and C appears as follows after the loss on the sale of the assets has been entered in the partners' capital account:

Balance Sheet

Cash	$220,000	Accounts payable	$10,000
		A, capital	110,000
		B, capital	90,000
		C, capital	10,000
Total	$220,000	Total	$220,000

The creditor must be paid in full before cash is distributed to the partners.

(1) Pay creditors	Accounts payable	10,000	
	Cash		10,000
(2) Pay partners	A, capital	110,000	
	B, capital	90,000	
	C, capital	10,000	
	Cash		210,000

Note that a profit-and-loss sharing ratio means just what the name indicates; it is a ratio for sharing profits or losses, not a ratio for sharing cash or any other assets. The amount of cash which a partner should receive in liquidation will be indicated by the balance in his or her capital account after the gain or loss from the disposal assets has been divided among the partners at the agreed ratio for sharing profits and losses.

Key Words and Phrases

admission	许可；接收
agency	代理
bankruptcy	破产
co-owner	共同拥有者
dissolve	解散
incapacity	无能力
liquidation	清算
mutual agency	互为代理
partner	合伙人
partnership	合伙
personal income tax	个人所得税
profit-and-loss sharing ratio	损益分配比率
sole proprietorship	独资
terminate	使结束
withdrawal	退出

Exercises

I. Fill in the blanks.

1. Business practice calls for a written agreement among the partners is called_____.

2. _____ is an association of two or more persons to carry on as co-owners a business for profit.

3. when a partnership goes out of business, it usually sells the assets, pays the creditors, and distributes the remaining cash or other assets to the partners. The process is called_____.

II. Computation.

1.X and Y invest $100,000 and $50,000 respectively in a partnership and agree to a division of net income that provides for an allowance of interest at 10% on original investments, salary allowances of $12,000 and $24,000 respectively, with the remainder divided equally. What would be X's share of a periodic net income of $45,000?

Reading Materials

Partnership accounting focuses on the business form that includes two or more principle owners within a business. The accounting process starts with calculating the value each partner has in the business. Income distribution is calculated using these percentages, unless the partnership agreement dictates something different. All partners have a specific ownership share in the assets, liabilities, and capital of the company. Each partner will have a withdrawal account he or she can use to take money legally out of the firm under partnership accounting.

An example of partnership accounting starts with Bill, Frank, and Suzie contributing $50,000 $30,000 and $20,000 respectively to their partnership. Classic partnership accounting rules dictate ownership percentage of 50 percent, 30 percent, and 20 percent for Bill, Frank, and Suzie. All future income distributions will fall under these percentages and be added to each partner's capital account in the firm. This income split allows each partner to maintain his or her ownership percentage in the firm as it grows.

Each partner's capital account represents a credit on the partnership's general <u>ledger</u>. To allocate income of $60,000, an accountant will debit the income account and distribute $30,000 to Bill's capital account, $18,000 to Frank's, and $12,000 to Suzie's. This increases each partner's value while keeping the initial ownership percentage the same. Partners can typically withdraw money from their capital account, but cannot reduce the initial capital balance; this would change the ownership percentages.

Partners may receive a paycheck for their contributions, similar to working as an employee in another firm. The paycheck will reduce the amount of income distributed to each partner. If each partner agrees to the same wage each month for services provided, the income at the end of each month will be lower. For example, if each partner agrees to a $4,000 monthly salary, the income allocation from the previous example will fall from $60,000 to $48,000. The income distribution will then follow the standard allocation method.

When a partner decides to leave the firm, the partnership will typically dissolve unless the initial agreement provides for a partner withdrawal. During the partnership accounting withdrawal process, the firm must revalue all assets and liabilities relating to the firm. The partner leaving the company will then receive his or her ownership percentage of the net assets in the firm. Accountants will add this figure to the partner's capital account and then pay the partner this amount when he or she leaves the firm.

Chapter 14　Corporation Accounting—Capital Stock

After studying this chapter, you should be able to:

- Understand characteristics of the corporation;
- Understand definition formation of corporation;
- Explain authorization and issuance of capital stock;
- Comprehend common stock and preferred stock;
- Understand treasury stock.

14.1　Characteristics of the Corporation

A corporation is an entity that is owned by its shareholders and raises equity capital by selling shares of stock to investors.

As a separate legal entity, it may own property in its own name, and it can incur debts, conduct business, enter into contracts and pay income taxes on its own earnings. The ownership of a corporation is divided into units called shares of stock. The owners of the shares are called stockholders or shareholders.

The owners of a corporation have limited liability. A corporation is responsible for its own acts and obligations under law. Therefore, a corporation's creditors usually may not go beyond the assets of the corporation to satisfy their claim. Thus, the financial loss that a stockholder may suffer is limited to the amount invested. The limited liability feature has contributed to the rapid growth of the corporate form of organization.

The transfer ability of ownership is another principal characteristic of the corporation stocks which represent the ownership to the corporation are highly liquid and can be transferred any time the owner wishes.

Stockholders exercise control over the management of a corporation's operation and activities by electing a board of directors. The board of directors meets periodically to establish corporate policies. The board selects the chief executive officer and other major officers to manage the day-to-day affairs of the corporation. The board also has responsibility for deciding when and how much corporate income to distribute to stockholders in the form of dividends.

14.2　Formation of a Corporation

The corporation must obtain a corporate charter from the state in which the corporation is formed, and it must receive authorization from that state to issue shares of capital stock.

Corporations are run by salaried professional managers, not by their stockholders. Thus the stockholders are primarily investors, rather than active participants in the business. The top level of a corporation's professional management is the board of directors. These directors are elected by the stockholders and responsible for hiring the other professional managers. In addition, the directors make major policy decisions, including the extent to profits of the corporation are distributed to stockholders. The fact that directors are elected by the stockholders means that a stockholder—or a group of stockholders—owning more than 50% of the company's stock effectively controls the corporation. These controlling stockholders have the voting power to elect the directors, who in turn set company policies and appoint manage and corporate officers.

A typical organizational chart of corporation is shown as follows:

Stockholders

Board of Directors

President

Professional Managers

14.2.1　Rights of Stockholders

A corporation is owned by its stockholder. Some companies issue more than one class of stocks, such as common stock and preferred stock. The interest of stockholder is determined by the number of shares that he or she owns.

The common stockholder in a corporation usually carries the following basic rights:

1. To vote for directors and on certain other key issues. Any stockholder or group of stockholders—who owns more than 50% of the capital stock—has the power to elect the board of directors and to set basic corporate policies. Therefore, these stockholders control the corporation.

2. To participate in any dividends declared by the board of directors. Dividends can be distributed only after they have been formally declared by the board of directors. Dividends are paid to all shareholders in proportion to the number of shares owned.

3. The right to share in the distribution of cash or other assets if the corporation is liquidated.

When a corporation ends its existence, the creditors of the corporation must first be paid in full; any remaining assets are divided among stockholders in proportion to the number of shares owned.

4. The right to maintain one's percentage ownership if the corporation increases the number of shares outstanding (called the preemptive right).

5. Stockholders' meetings usually are held once a year. Each share of stocks is entitled to one vote. In large corporation, these annual meetings are usually attended by relatively a few persons, often by less than 1% of the stockholders. Prior to the meeting, the management group will request stockholders who do not attend in person to send in proxy statements assigning their votes to the existing management. Through this proxy system, management may secure the right to vote as much as, perhaps, 90% or more of the total outstanding shares.

14.2.2 Stockholders' Equity

The sections of the balance sheet showing assets and labilities are much the same for all three forms of business organization. The owners' equity section is the principal point of contrast. In the balance sheet of a corporation, the term stockholders' equity is used instead of owners' equity. Stockholders' equity consists of legal capital—par or stated amounts received from the sale and issuance of capital stock. The total par or stated value of all issued stock constitutes the legal capital of corporation. Common stocks and preferred stocks are the two classes of capital stocks. And retained earnings which is the net income accumulated since the operation of a corporation and not distributed to the shareholders.

14.3 Equity Accounting for the Corporation

Accounting for the corporation is distinguished from accounting for the sole proprietorship or the partnership or the partnership by the treatment of owners' equity, which in the corporation is separated into paid-in capital and retained earnings. The reason for this separation is that most states prohibit corporations from paying dividends from other than retained earnings. Paid-in capital is further divided and so we have three major capital accounts.

Capital stock (paid-in capital or contributed capital). This account shows the par value of the stock issued by the corporation. It is recorded in separate accounts for each class of stock.

Additional Paid-in Capital. This account shows the amounts paid in beyond the par value of stock.

Retained Earnings. This account shows the accumulated earnings arising from profitable operation of the business.

14.4　Authorization and Issuance of Capital Stock

The articles of incorporation specify the number of shares of capital stock which a corporation is authorized to issue and the par value. The corporation may not choose to issue immediately all the authorized shares; in fact, it is customary to secure authorization for a larger number of shares than presently needed. In future years, if more capital is needed, the preciously authorized shares will be readily available for issue; otherwise, the corporation would be forced to apply to the state for permission to increase the number of authorized shares.

14.4.1　Authorization of Stock

In issuing stock, the stock must be authorized by the government. The number of shares the corporation can issue is called authorized shares. Issued stock is the stock that has been sold to a stockholder and for which a stock certificate has been issued. Outstanding stock is the stock that is in the hand of a stockholder. Not all issued stock is outstanding. Corporations may buy their stock back; this stock, that is treasury stock, which has been issued but not outstanding.

The relationship among authorized shares, issued shares and outstanding shares shows as follows:

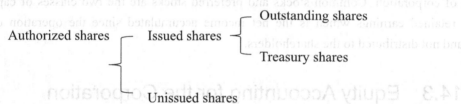

In Chinese practice, we use legal capital system. Legal capital is specified in China as the par value of the authorized shares. In China, issued shares should equal to the authorized shares. Maintenance of legal capital means that a corporation must retrain from paying dividends when their effect would impair legal capital. Legal capital can be impaired as a result of operating losses. Further, currently Chinese corporation law prohibits corporation from buying treasury stock. Due to these situations, in Chinese practice, the authorized shares equal to issue shares whose number is the same as that of outstanding shares.

14.4.2　Par Value

The chief significance of par value is that it represents the legal per share. There is no necessary relationship between the price at which a corporation issues stock, and the price at which the stocks trades in the marketplace, and the par value of the stock. If a corporation issues par value stock at a price in excess of par, the stock is said to be issued at a premium.

If a corporation issues stock at a price below par value, the stock is said to be issued at a discount. Investors who purchase shares from a corporation at a price equal to or exceeding par value can not lose more than their investment. Investors who acquire shares at a discount may lose their original investment plus an amount equal to the account.

14.5   Classes of Shares

14.5.1   Common Stocks

Common shares are known as the residual class because common shareholders claims to assets and profits of a business rank behind those of creditors and preferred shareholders. The stockholders, as owners of the business, have the right to vote, to share in profits, to transfer ownership and to share in the distribution of assets in case of liquidation.

A share of stock represents a unit of the stockholders' interest in the business. The par value of a stock is an arbitrary amount established in the corporation's charter and printed on the face of each stock certificate. It bears no relation to the market value, that is, the current purchase or selling price. There are several categories of stock shares showing below.

Authorized shares are shares of stock which a corporation is permitted to issue (sell) under its articles of incorporation.

Unissued shares are authorized shares which have not yet been offered for sale.

Subscribed shares are shares which a buyer has contracted to purchase at a specific price on a certain date. The shares will not be issued until full payment has been received.

Treasury stock represents shares which have been and later reacquired by the corporation.

Outstanding stock represents shares authorized, issued and in the hands of stockholders. (Treasury stock is not outstanding, as it belongs to the corporation and not to the stockholders.)

14.5.2   Preferred Stock

Stocks that carry certain specified preferences, or first claim, are called preferred stock. Usually these preferences show as follows:

1. Preference as to dividends. Shares with a dividend preference entitle their owners to receive dividends of a certain amount.

2. Preference as to assets. Shares with a liquidating preference entitle the holders to receive a certain amount, in the event the corporation liquidates, before shares with secondary preference or no preference receive anything.

14.5.3   Classes of Preferred Stock

1. Stock preferred as to dividends. Stock preferred as to dividends is entitled to receive each year a dividend of specified amount before any dividend is paid to the common stock. The

dividend is usually stated as a dollar amount per share. Some preferred stocks state the dividend preference as a percentage of par values.

2. Cumulative preferred stock. Preferred stock on which the claims for dividends may be accumulated from year to year is called cumulative preferred stock. If the directors do not declare the dividend in any year, the unpaid amount will accumulate until it is paid out of the earnings of subsequent years.

3. Noncumulative preferred stock. The preferred stock on which the claim for dividends do not accumulate from year to year is called noncumulative preferred stock. The holder of noncumulative preferred stock is only entitled to receive dividends if the earnings for the year are sufficient to pay such dividends and if the board of directors declares them.

4. Full participating preferred stock. A full participating preferred stock is one which in addition to the regular specified dividend, is entitled to participate in any additional dividend paid as the common stock.

5. Stock preferred as to assets. Most preferred stocks carry a preference as to cash and other assets in the event of liquidation of the corporation. If the business is terminated, the preferred stock is entitled to payment in full of its par value or a higher stated liquidation value before any payment is made to the common stock.

6. Callable preferred stock. Most preferred stocks include a call provision. This provision grants the issuing corporation the right to repurchase the stock from the stockholders at a stipulated call price.

7. Convertible preferred stock. In order to add to the attractiveness of preferred stock as an investment, corporation sometimes offers a conversion privilege which entitles the preferred stockholders to exchange their shares for common stock at a stipulated ratio.

14.6   Issue of Stock

14.6.1   Stock Issuing at Par

A separate account is used for recording the amount of each class of stock issued to investors in a corporation.

【Example 14.1】Issuing at par

Assume that Caldwell corporation is authorized to issue 10,000 shares of preferred stock, $100 par, and 100,000 shares of common stock, $20 par. One-half of each class of authorized shares is issued at par for cash.

Cash	1,500,000	
Preferred Stock		500,000
Common Stock		1,000,000

The stock accounts (preferred stock, common stock) are controlling accounts. A record of each stockholders' name, address and number of shares held is normally kept in a subsidiary ledger. This subsidiary ledger is called the stockholders ledger. It provides the information for issuing dividend checks, annual meeting notices, and financial reports to individual stockholders.

14.6.2   Stock Issuing at Premium

When stock is issued for a price that is higher than its par, the stock has sold at a premium. When stock is issued for a price that is lower than its par, the stock has sold at a discount. Thus, if stock with a par of $50 is issued for a price of $60, the stock has sold at a premium of $10. If the same stock is issued for a price of $45, the stock has sold at a discount of $5. Many states do not permit the issuance of stock at a discount. In others, it may be done only under unusual conditions. Since issuing stock at a discount is rare, we will not illustrate it.

When stock is issued at a premium, cash or other asset accounts are debited for the amount received. The stock account is then credited for the par amount. The excess of the amount paid over par is a part of the total investment of the stockholders in the corporation. Therefore, such an amount in excess of par should be classified as a part of the paid-in capital. An account entitled paid-in capital in excess of par is usually credited for this amount.

【Example 14.2】 **Issuing a premium**

Caldwell corporation issues 2,000 shares of $50 par preferred stock for cash at $55.

Cash	110,000	
Preferred stock		100,000
Paid-in capital in excess of par-preferred stock		10,000

When stock is issued in exchange for assets other than cash, such as land, buildings and equipment, the assets acquired should be recorded at their fair market value. If the fair market value of the assets can not be objectively determined, the fair market price of the stock issued may be used.

【Example 14.3】 Caldwell corporation acquired land for which the fair market value can not be determined. In exchange, the corporation issued 10,000 shares of its $10 par common stock. Assuming the stock has a current market price of $12 per share, the transaction is recorded as follows:

Land	120,000	
Common stock		100,000
Paid-in capital in excess of par		20,000

14.7   Treasury Stock

Treasury stock is a corporation's own stock that has been issued and subsequently reacquired by purchases. The firm may reacquire its shares for a number of reasons: to obtain shares that can be used in the future for acquisitions, bonus plans, exercise of warrants, and conversion of convertible bonds or preferred stocks; to increase the earnings per share and therefore the market price of each share; to thwart an attempt by outsider to accumulate shares in anticipation of a takeover attempt; or to increase the market price of each share of the stock.

A commonly used method of accounting for the purchase and the resale of treasury stock is the cost method. When the stock is purchased by the corporation, the account treasury stock is debited for its cost. The par value and the price at which the stock was originally issued are ignored. When the stock is resold, treasury stock is credited for its cost, and any difference between the cost and the selling price is normally debited or credited to a paid-in capital account. This latter account is entitled paid-in capital from sale of treasury stock.

【Example 14.4】 Assume that the paid-in capital of Caldwell corporation is as follows:

Common stock, $25 par	
(20,000 shares authorized and issued)	$500,000
Excess of issue price over par	150,000
	$650,000

The transaction involving treasury stock and the related entries are as follows:

1. Purchased 1,000 shares of treasury stock at $45

Treasury stock	45,000	
Cash		45,000

2. Sold 200 shares of treasury stock at $60

Cash	12,000	
Treasury stock		9,000
Paid-in capital from sale of treasury stock		3,000

3. Sold 200 shares of treasury stock at $40

Cash	8,000	
Paid-in capital from sale of treasury stock	1,000	
Treasury stock		9,000

As illustrated, a sale of treasury stock may result in a decrease in paid-in capital. To the extent that paid-in capital from sale of treasury stock has a credit balance, it should be debited for any decrease. Any remaining decrease should then be debited to the retained earnings account.

Key Words and Phrases

additional paid-in capital	资本公积
authorized shares	已授股权
capital stock	股本
chief executive officer	执行总裁
common stocks	普通股

contributed capital	实缴资本
convertible preferred stock	可转换优先股
cumulative preferred stock	累积优先股
equity capital	权益资本
outstanding stock	已公开发行并售出股
participating preferred stock	参与优先股
par value	面值
preferred stocks	优先股
treasury stock	库藏股
unissued shares	未发行股

Exercises

I. Fill in the blanks.

1. _____ is the capital contributed to the corporation by the stockholders and others.

2. _____ is the amount of prior net income that the firm had retained.

3. _____ are superior to common stock with respect to dividends.

4. _____ can be exchanged for common shares at the preferred shareholders' option.

5. _____ is a corporation's own stock that has been issued stock and subsequently reacquired by purchases.

6. The amount paid in excess of par by a purchaser of newly issued stock is called a _____.

7. If a corporation issues only one class of stock, this stock is known as _____.

II. Computation.

Assume that Caldwell corporation has 1,000 shares of $4 nonparticipating preferred stock and 4,000 shares of common stock outstanding. Also assume that the net income, amount of earnings retained had been decided.

	First year	Second year	Third year
Net income	20,000	55,000	100,000
Amount distributed			
Preferred divided			
Common divided			
Amount retained	10,000	20,000	40,000
Divided per share:			
Preferred			
Common			

Reading Materials

What is capital stock?

Capital stock has to do with all the shares of stock that represent the ownership of a given company. The exact number of shares that can be issued in the way of capital stock is normally recorded in the current balance sheet for a company. Capital stock will involve all types or classes of stock that the company is authorized to issue.

The basis for issuing capital stock is normally outlined in the charter of the <u>corporation</u>. Often, the charter will specify not only the number of shares that can be included as part of the issuance, but also define the class or classes of stock that the corporation will release for issue. It is not unusual for a company to issue both common stock along with preferred stock as part of the overall strategy. The common stock may be provided to hourly employees of the company as part of the benefit package, while the preferred stock is open for issue to any outside investor.

Generally, capital stock is issued at a nominal value, but may increase in value over time. There is also the possibility of additional shares of capital stock coming available as the company expands its operations and begins to realize higher profits. When this happens, it is necessary for current investors to work with board members to amend the charter of the company, making it legal to issue more shares of stock. At the same time, the company must work within the financial laws currently in place in the country of jurisdiction to determine the maximum number of shares that the company can publicly trade.

The charter of the company will also address the total value of stock that can be issued. This total value will of course impact the number of shares of capital stock that the corporation can issue under current circumstances. Generally, when the charter is amended and the Articles of Association updated, existing stockholders are notified and given the opportunity to purchase the newly issued shares on the open market.

Chapter 15　An Overview of Financial Management

After studying this chapter, you should be able to:

- Understand the career opportunities in finance;
- Explain financial staff's responsibilities;
- Master the goals of the corporation.

15.1　Career Opportunities in Finance

Finance consists of three interrelated areas: (1) money and capital market, which deals with securities markets and financial institutions; (2) investments, which focuses on the decisions made by both individual and institutional investors as they choose securities for their investment portfolios; and (3) financial management, or " business finance", which involves decisions within firms. The career opportunities within each field are numerous and varied, but financial managers must have knowledge of all three areas if they are to do their jobs well.

15.1.1　Money and Capital Market

Many finance majors go to work for financial institutions, including banks, insurance companies, mutual funds, and investment banking firms. For success here, one needs a knowledge of valuation techniques, the factors that cause interest rates to rise and fall, the regulations to which financial institutions are subject, and the various types of financial instruments (mortgages, auto loans, certificates of deposit, etc). One also needs a general knowledge of all aspects of business administration, because the management of a financial institution involves accounting, marketing, personnel, and computer system, as well as financial management. An ability to communicate, both orally and in writing, is important, and "people skills", or the ability to get others to do their jobs well, are critical.

One common entry-level job in this area is a bank officer trainee, where one goes into banks operations and learns about the business, from tellers, to cash management, to making loans. One could expect to spend a year or so being rotated among these different areas, after which he or she would settle into a department, often as an assistant manager in a branch. Alternatively, one might become a specialist in some area such as real estate, and be authorized to make loans going into millions of dollars, or in the management of trusts, estates, and pension funds. Similar career paths are available with insurance companies, investment companies, credit unions and consumer loan companies.

15.1.2　Investments

Finance graduates whom go into investment often work for a brokerage house such as Merrill Lynch, either in sales or as a security analyst. Others work for banks mutual funds, or insurance companies in the management of their investment portfolios; for financial consulting firms advising individual investors or pension funds on how to invest their capital; for an investment bank whose primary function is to help businesses raise new capital; or as financial planners whose job is to help individuals develop long-term financial goals and portfolios. The three main functions in the investments area are sales, analyzing individual securities, and determining the optimal mix of securities for a given investor.

15.1.3　Financial Management

Financial management is the broadest of the three areas, and the one with the most job opportunities. Financial management is important in all types of businesses, including banks and other financial institutions, as well as industrial and retail firms. Financial management is also important in governmental operations, from schools to hospitals to highway departments. The job opportunities in financial management range from making decisions regarding plant expansions to choosing what types of securities to issue when financing expansion. Financial managers also have the responsibility for deciding the credit terms under which customers may buy, how much inventory the firm should carry, how much cash to keep on hand, whether to acquire other firms, and how much of the firm's earnings to plow back into the business versus pay out as dividends.

Regardless of which area a finance major goes into, he or she will need a knowledge of all three areas. For example, a bank lending officer can not do this or her job well without a good understanding of financial management, because he or she must be able to judge how well a business is being operated. The same thing holds true for Merrill Lynch's security analysts and stockbrokers, who must have an understanding of general financial principles if they are to give their customers intelligent advice. Similarly, corporate financial managers need to know what their bankers are thinking about, and they also need to know how investors judge a firm's performance and thus determine its stock price. So if you decide to make finance as your career, you will need to know something about all three areas.

But suppose you do not plan to major in finance. Is the subject still important to you? Absolutely, for two reasons: (1) you need a knowledge of finance to make many personal decisions, ranging from investing for your retirement to deciding whether to lease versus buy a car; (2) virtually all important business decisions have financial implications, so important decisions are generally made by teams from the accounting, finance, legal, marketing, personnel, and production department. Therefore, if you want to succeed in the business arena, you must be highly competent in your own area, say, marketing, but you must also have a familiarity with other business disciplines, including finance.

Thus, there are financial implications in virtually all business decisions, and nonfinancial executives simply must know enough finance to work these implications into their own specialized analyses. Because of this, every student of business, regardless of his or her major, should be concerned with financial management.

15.2 The Financial Staff's Responsibilities

The financial staff's task is to acquire and then help operate resources so as to maximize the value of the firm. Here are some specific activities.

15.2.1 Forecasting and Planning

The financial staff must coordinate the planning process. This means they must interact with people from other departments as they look ahead and lay the plans that will shape the firm's future.

15.2.2 Major Investment and Financing Decisions

A successful firm usually has rapid growth in sales, which requires investments in plant, equipment and inventory. The financial staff must help determine the optional sales growth rate, help decide what specific assets to acquire, and then choose the best way to finance those assets. For example, should the firm finance with debt, equity, or some combination of the two, and if debt is used, how much should be long-term and how much short-term?

15.2.3 Coordination and Control

The financial staff must interact with other personnel to ensure that the firm is operated as efficiently as possible. All business decisions have financial implications and all mangers — financial and otherwise — need to take this into account. For example, marketing decisions affect sales growth, which in turn influences investment requirements. Thus, marketing decision makers must take account of how their actions affect and are affected by such factors as the availability of funds, inventory polities, and plant capacity utilization.

15.2.4 Dealing with Financial Markets

The financial staff must deal with the money and capital markets. Each firm affects and is affected by the general financial markets where funds are raised, where the firm's securities are traded, and where investors whether make or lose money.

15.2.5　Risk Management

All businesses face risks, including natural disasters such as fires and floods, uncertainties in commodity and securities markets, volatile interest rates, and fluctuation foreign exchange rates. However, many of these risks can be reduced by purchasing insurance or by hedging in the derivatives markets. The financial staff is responsible for the firm's overall risk management program, including identifying the risks that should be managed and then managing them in the most efficient manner.

In summary, people working in financial management make decisions regarding which assets their firms should require, how those assets should be financed, and how the firm should conduct its operations. If these responsibilities are performed optimally, financial managers will help to maximize the values of their firms, and this will also contribute to the welfare of consumers and employees.

15.3　The Goals of the Corporation

Shareholders are owners of a corporation, and they purchase stocks because they are looking for a financial return. In most cases, shareholders elect directors, who then hire managers on behalf of shareholders. It follows that they should pursue policies that enhance shareholder value. Consequently, we assume that management's primary goal is stockholder's wealth maximization, which translates into maximizing the price of the firm's common stock. Firms do, of course, have other objectives. In particular, the managers who make the actual decisions are interested in their own personal satisfaction, in their employees' welfare, and in the good of the community and of society at large. Still, for reasons set forth in the following sections, stock price maximizations are the most important goal for most corporations.

15.3.1　Managerial Incentives to Maximize Shareholder Wealth

Because the stock of most large firms is widely held, managers of large corporations have a great deal of autonomy. This being the case, might not managers pursue goals other than stock price maximizations. For example, some have argued that the managers of large, well-entrenched corporations could work just hard enough to keep stockholder returns at a "reasonable" level and then devote the remainder of their effort and resources to public service activities, to employee benefits, to higher executive salaries.

It is almost impossible to determine whether a particular management team is trying to maximize shareholder wealth or is merely attempting to keep stockholders satisfied while managers pursue other goals. For example, how can we tell whether employee or community benefit programs are in the long-run best interests of the stockholders? Similarly, are huge executive salaries really necessary to attract and retain excellent managers, or are they just another example of manager taking advantage of stockholders?

It is impossible to give definitive answers to these questions. However, we do know that the managers of a firm operating in a competitive market will be forced to undertake actions that are reasonable consistent with shareholder wealth maximization. If they depart from that goal, they run the risk of being removed from their jobs, either by the firm's board of directors or by outside forces.

15.3.2   Stock Price Maximization and Social Welfare

If a firm attempts to maximize its stock price, is this good or bad for society? In general, it is good. Aside from such illegal actions as attempting to form monopoles, violating safety codes, and failing to meet pollution control requirements, the same actions that maximize stock prices also benefit society.

First, note that stock price maximization requires efficient, low-cost businesses that produce high-quality goods and services at the lowest possible cost.

Second, stock price maximization requires the development of products and services that consumers want and need, so the profit motive leads to new technology, to new products, and to new jobs.

Finally, stock price maximization necessitates efficient and courteous service, adequate stocks of merchandise, and well-located business establishments. These are the factors that leads to sales, which in turn are necessary for profits.

Therefore, most actions that help a firm increase the price of its stock also benefit society at large. This is why profit-motivated, free-enterprise economies have been so much more successful than socialistic and communistic economic systems. Since financial management has played a crucial role in the operations of successful firms, and since successful firms have been absolutely necessary for a healthy, productive economy, it is easy to see why finance is important from a social welfare standpoint.

Key Words and Phrases

board of directors	董事会
business administration	企业管理
finance majors	从事金融业务人员
financial instruments	金融工具
financial management	财务管理
financial markets	金融市场
financial staff	财务人员

financing decisions	融资决策
maximize shareholder wealth	股东财富最大化
money and capital markets	货币和资本市场
rates of return on investment	投资报酬率
risk management	风险管理
shareholder	股东
stockholder	股东

Exercises

I. Fill in the blanks.

1. Finance consists of three interrelated areas: _____, _____, _____.

2. Many _____ go to work for financial institutions, including banks, insurance companies, mutual funds, and investment banking firms.

3. _____ the most important goal for most corporations.

4. Stockholders own the firm and elect_____, which then selects the management team.

5. _____ have costs, and not all businesses would voluntarily incur all such costs.

II. Answer the following questions.

1. What are some specific activities in which a firm finance staff is involved?

2. What are the three main areas of finance?

3. Why is it necessary for business students who do not plan to major in finance to understand the basics of finance?

4. If a firm attempts to maximize its stock price, is this good or bad for society?

Reading Materials

Financial Management

Financial management refers to the efficient and effective management of money (funds) in such a manner as to accomplish the objectives of the organization. It is the specialized function directly associated with the top management. The significance of this function is not only seen in the 'Line' but also in the capacity of 'Staff' in overall of a company. It has been defined differently by different experts in the field.

The term typically applies to an organization or company's financial strategy, while personal finance or financial life management refers to an individual's management strategy. It includes how to raise the capital and how to allocate capital, i.e. capital budgeting. Not only for long term budgeting, but also how to allocate the short-term resources like current liabilities. It also deals with the dividend policies of the shareholders.

Objectives of Financial Management

- Profit maximization occurs when marginal cost is equal to marginal revenue. This is the main objective of financial management.
- Wealth maximization means maximization of shareholders' wealth. It is an advanced goal compared to profit maximization.
- Survival of company is an important consideration when the financial manager makes any financial decisions. One incorrect decision may lead company to be bankrupt.
- Maintaining proper cash flow is a short run objective of financial management. It is necessary for operations to pay the day-to-day expenses e.g. raw material, electricity bills, wages, rent etc. A good cash flow ensures the survival of company.
- Minimization on capital cost in financial management can help operations gain more profit.

Scope of Financial Management

- Estimating the Requirement of Funds: Businesses make forecast on funds needed in both short run and long run, hence, they can improve the efficiency of funding. The estimation is based on the budget e.g. sales budget, production budget.
- Determining the Capital Structure: Capital structure is how a firm finances its overall operations and growth by using different sources of funds. Once the requirement of funds has estimated, the financial manager should decide the mix of debt and equity and also types of debt.
- Investment Fund: A good investment plan can bring businesses huge returns.

Financial Management for Start Up

For new enterprises, it is important to make a good estimation on costs and sales. Consideration on appropriate length sources of finances can help businesses avoid the cash flow problems even the failure of setting up. There are fixed and current sides of assets balance sheet. Fixed assets refers to assets that cannot be converted into cash easily, like plant, property, equipment etc. A current asset is an item on an entity's balance sheet that is either cash, a cash equivalent, or which can be converted into cash within one year. It is not easy for start ups to forecast the current asset, because there are changes in receivables and payables.

Chapter 16　Analysis of Financial Statements

After studying this chapter, you should be able to:

- Explain the basic financial statement analysis;
- Calculate accounting ratios and know how these ratios are used to analyze financial statements;
- Develop the ability to analyze the financial statements of an organization;
- Describe the importance of financial analysis when making decisions.

16.1　Introduction to Financial Statement Analysis

Financial statement analysis is the examination of both the relationships among financial statement numbers and the trends in those numbers over time. One purpose of financial statement analysis is to use the past performance of a company to predict its future profitability and cash flows. Another purpose of financial statement analysis is to evaluate the performance of a company with an eye toward identifying problem areas. In other words, financial statement analysis is both diagnoses, identifying where a firm has problems, and prognosis, predicting how a firm will perform in the future.

Much information can be obtained about a company's status from its financial statements, but trends of ratios can give a more accurate impression of where a company is going. By rearranging information from financial statements people can get information about the following areas of financial performance: (1) short-term liquidity; (2) long-term solvency and capital structure; (3) profitability; (4) efficiency; (5) growth. Financial statements cannot directly provide the answer to the preceding five measures of performance. However, management must constantly evaluate how well the firm is doing. Financial ratios are calculated to provide the information.

Financial ratios express relationships between certain components of the financial statements. When used properly, ratio analysis is a powerful tool for unraveling the underlying reasons for the financial structure, condition and trends of a business. Ration analysis can also mislead, especially if ratios are taken at face value on a stand-alone basis, instead of being related to other ratios and to the vast array of other information available on a business.

16.2 Ratio Analysis

Once you understand how a set of accounts is constructed, you need to be able to analyze them to find out what they really disclose. Interpreting and analyzing financial statements will enable you, as a manager, to compare the performance of your company this year with last year, to compare your company with its competitors, and to detect weaknesses which you can improve.

Absolute figures in financial statements do not tell you much. For example, to be told that retail stores Hongxin made $200 million profits before tax is not a useful piece of information unless it is related to, say, the turnover which produced the profit or to the capital employed in the group.

Ratio analysis is a useful tool with which to interpret financial accounts. But for ratios to be meaningful, they must be compared with equivalent ratios calculated for previous years and with those of the industry in which the company is positioned. Industrial ratios are produced by a variety of clearing houses for industrial statistics.

Ratios reduce the amount of data contained in the financial statements to workable form. This aim is defeated if too many are calculated. You must learn which combination of ratios will be appropriate to your needs.

16.3 Detailed Ratios

Ratios are used extensively in the interpretation of financial statements and, when calculated, the comparisons are made.

16.3.1 Short-term Liquidity

Ratios of short-term liquidity measure the ability of the firm to meet recurring financial obligations. To the extent a firm has sufficient cash-flow, it will be able to avoid defaulting on its financial obligations and, thus, avoid experiencing financial distress. The basic source from which to pay current liabilities are current assets. The most widely used measures of accounting liquidity are shown in Table 16-1.

Table 16-1 Liquidity Ratios

Content	Formula
Current ratio	Total current assets / total current liabilities
Quick ratio	Quick assets / total current liabilities
Account receivable turn	Sales / accounts receivable
Payable turn	Cost of goods sold / account payable

续表

Content	Formula
Inventory turn	Cost of goods sold/ inventory
Days' stock on hand	Ending inventory/ cost of goods sold × 365
Amount of working capital	Current assets / current liability

16.3.2　Long-term Solvency and Capital Structure

An analysis of working capital evaluates the short-term liquidity of the company. However, analysts are also interested in a company's ability to meet its obligations and provide securing to its creditors over the long run. The main ratios are as follows in Table 16-2.

Table 16-2　Ratios about Long-term Solvency and Capital Structure

Content	Formula
Net worth to total assets	Total share holders equity / total assets
Debt ratio	Total debt / total assets
Equity multiplier	Total assets / total equity
Interest overage	Earnings before interest and taxes / interest expense
Capitalization ratio	Long term debt / (long term debt+ owners' equity)
Debt to equity ratio	Total debt / total equity

16.3.3　Profitability

One of the most difficult attributes of a firm to conceptualize and to measure is profitability. In general sense, accounting profits are the difference between revenues and cost. Unfortunately, there is no completely unambiguous way to know when a firm is profitable. At best, a financial analyst can measure current or past accounting profitability. Many business opportunities, however, involve sacrificing current profits for future profits. Thus, current profits can be a poor reflection of true future profitability. Another problem with accounting based measures of profitability is that it ignores risk. The most important conceptual problem with accounting measures of profitability is they do not give us a benchmark for making comparisons. The ratios are as follows in Table 16-3.

Table 16-3　Ratios of Profitability

Content	Formula
Net profit margin	Net income / total operating revenue
Gross profit margin	EBIT / total operating revenues
Operating margin	Operating income / sales
ROI	Net income / average owners' equity

Content	Formula
ROA	Net income/ average total assets
ROE	Net income/average stockholders' equity

16.3.4 Efficiency

Financial analysts are especially interested in the ability of a company to use its assets efficiency to produce profits for its owners and thus provide cash flows to them.

Total asset turnover = net sales / total assets: this ratio helps the analyst appraise the overall efficiency of asset employment and the level of capital intensity. The higher the ratio, the more efficient in managing and controlling assets is.

Fixed asset turnover = net sales / average fixed assets: this ratio shows the numbers in dollars in sales during the year generated by each dollar of fixed assets.

16.3.5 Growth

Past and expected growth rates of a company's sales, profits, assets and etc are a major focus of many financial statement analyses. Investors are interested because of the close relationship between equity stock values and the projected growth rate and the expected volatility of earnings and dividends. Creditors examine past growth records in order to predict the future level of funding required to finance changes in accounts receivables, inventories, and productive assets.

They are sales growth, profit growth, asset growth and equity growth.

The sustainable growth rate = ROE × retention ratio: this ratio is the maximum rate of growth a firm can maintain without increasing its financial leverage and using internal equity only.

16.4 The Limitations of Ratio Analysis

Ratios will suffer from the same deficiencies as the information from which they are calculated. The financial statements of most organizations have some drawbacks.

16.4.1 Historical Cost Accounting

The financial statements of most organizations are drawn up using the historical cost concept. Little or no account is taken of inflation, which invariably leads to undervalued assets on the Balance Sheet. Also many companies do not include a value for intangible assets such as goodwill on their Balance Sheet.

This will have a particularly distorting effect on the ratios that use fixed asset figures.

16.4.2 Seasonal Fluctuations

The level of activity of many organizations varies on a seasonal basis. The Balance Sheet lists the assets and liabilities of an organization on one day of the year only and, therefore, the assets and liabilities may not be representative of the year as a whole.

16.4.3 Non-standardization of Accounting Policies

Despite the growing number of accounting standard, there is still considerable scope for organizations to adopt their own accounting policies, e.g., different methods of calculating depreciation. The adoption of different accounting policies makes inter-firm comparison difficult.

Key Words and Phrases

financial statement analysis	财务报表分析
due	到期的
rate of return	回报率
trend analysis	趋势分析
ratio analysis	比率分析
accounting policies	会计政策
investment income	投资收益
profitability ratio	盈利能力比率
return on capital employed	投资回报率
return on net assets	净资产报酬率
net profit ratio	销售净利率
gross profit margin	销售毛利率
overheads to sales ratio	间接费用与销售比率
dividend yield	股利收益率
earnings per share	每股收益
price earnings ratio	市盈率
liquidity ratio	流动能力比率
current ratio	流动比率
quick ratio	速动比率
stock turnover	存货周转率
debtor's collection period	应收账款收账期
creditor's payment period	应付账款付款期
working capital	营运资本
cash budgeting	现金预算

fixed to current asset ratio	固定资产对流动资产比率
debt ratio	资产负债率
times interest earned	利息保障倍数
fixed assets turnover	固定资产周转率
dividend cover	股利保证倍数

Exercises

I. Fill in the blanks.

1. _____ report both on a firm's position at a point in time and on its operations over some past period.

2. Two commonly used liquidity ratios are _____ and _____.

3. The second group of ratios, _____, measures how effectively the firm is managing its assets.

4. _____ measures the extent to which operating income can decline before the firm is unable to meet its annual interest costs.

5. _____ show the combined effects of liquidity, asset management, and debt on operating results.

6. _____ give management an indication of what investors think of the company's past performance and future prospects.

II. Make word combinations using a word from each box. One word can be used twice. Then use the word combinations to complete the sentences below.

Acid
Current
Dividend
Liquid
Quick

Assets
Cover
Ratio
Test

1. (_____) consist of cash and things that can be easily sold and converted to cash.

2. A high (_____) shows that the company is retaining a lot of money belonging to its shareholders.

3. The (_____) shows a company's ability to pay its short-term debts.

III. Match the two parts of the sentences.

1. If a company pays out retained surpluses from past years
2. Some investors are worried that the new stock issue
3. A high current ratio indicates short-term financial strength but
4. Wall street is on a historical price-earnings ratio of around 35, which

a. it does not measure how efficiently the company is utilizing its resources.

b. its dividend cover will fall below 1.0.

c. makes the market very expensive, as the long-term average is 14.45.

d. will dilute the company's earnings per share.

Reading Materials

Target Costing: A Strategic Profit Management System

Target costing supposedly originated in Japan in the 1960s, where it is known as Genka Kikaku. It is not a costing system but could be considered a profit planning system as it is a comprehensive system to control costs and manager profit over a product's life cycle—from the product concept to the sale of the last spare part years after the product has ceased production. Kato(1993) described the target costing this way:

Target costing is an activity which is aimed at reducing the life-cycle costs of new products, while ensuring quality, reliability, and other consumer requirements, by examining all possible ideas for cost reduction at the product planning, research and development, and the prototyping phases of production. But it is not just a cost reduction technique; it is part of a comprehensive strategic profit management system.

Target costing is an important tool because it promotes cost consciousness and focuses on profit margins, both of which strengthen an organization's competitive position. It is not a technique that attempts to slash costs by trimming functions or closing departments; it is a steady and never-ending pressure to make sure that costs are always kept to a minimum. It is entirely different from standard costing where managers are expected to keep within predetermined standard costs, and variances are calculated to determine whether they have done so.

Standard costing, as used in the West, does not start with the product concept. Instead it starts as the product goes into production with a predetermined set of circumstances. That is: the organization is going to make a new product, it will be designed this particular way and as a consequence the costs will be so much, and this in turn influences the selling price.

Target costing, as used in East, starts with a product design concept. From this a selling price is determined for the product and a profit requirement is set. This leads to the development of a target costs, this is the cost that must be met if profit is going to be achieved. Finally the product is designed to achieve the target cost-if this is not possible aspects of the product would be redesigned until the target is met.

The target profit requirement, of say 15%, should be driven by strategic profit planning rather than a standard mark-up. In Japan, this is done after consideration of the medium-term profit plans which reflect management and business strategies over that period. Once it is set the target profit is not just an expectation; it is a commitment agreed by all the people who have any part in achieving it. Therefore, the procedures used to derive a target profit must be scientific, rational and agreed by all staff responsible for achieving it otherwise no one will accept responsibility for achieving it.

Although both approaches use predetermined measures as controls, the difference between them is absolutely fundamental. The Western approach is always short-term cost control through variance analysis, with no medium-term planning of costs that tie the operational to the long-term strategic plans.

The use of target costing rectifies this weakness as the medium-term strategic position is considered at the start of the process with the product concept and the determination of the required profit. If it is thought that the product cannot generate the required profit it will not be produced. Target costing continues over the product's life and the pressure to reduce costs is continuous as costs are reduced monthly. This is another difference between target and standard costing where standards are often only revised annually.

The target costing approach is a vital total cost control tool because research has shown that up to 90% of costs are "built in" at the product's design stage. For example, the design stage sets the following:

- The design specification of the product including extra features. For example, the specification may be for a basic car with lots of additional extras that may be specified and paid for separately. Alternatively it may be for a product that includes as standard most of the extras desired by customers. Clearly the latter car will be cheaper, but does it meet customer requirements better?

- The number of components incorporated in the product. For example, during an anti-dumping argument in the 1980s, the EU accused Amstrad of dumping their audio systems in Europe, which is, selling them at a price less than cost. During a television debate on this, the cover was taken off a Grundig and an Amstrad machine. The former was considerably more expensive and no doubt produced a far better sound for those with discerning ears. The Grundig case was full of wires, soldered elements, etc., and to the untutored eye was a confusing mass of many different parts the Amstrad case was half empty. Was this because the designers thought that customers would perceive the product to be inferior if it were smaller? About a quarter of the space was occupied by a box, a single component, to which some wires were attached, anyone could see that it would be a lot cheaper to produce because assembly time would be only a fraction of the Grundig machine.

- Design of components. These should be designed for reliability in use and ease of manufacture. Possible standard parts should be used, because they are proven to be reliable and will help reduce stock and handling costs. Where new components are required it is important that their manufacturing process is considered before the component is finally designed so that they can be manufactured as cheaply as possible consistent with quality and functionality.

- Type of packaging required. This includes product packaging and packing per case and per pallet. The aim is to protect the product and to minimize handling costs by not breaking pallets or cases during distribution.

- The number of spare parts that need to be carried. This ties in with the number of components used. Parts must sometimes be held for up to 15 years ago. They may be made while the product is still in production and stored for years, which is costly. The alternative is to disrupt current production to make a small batch of a past component, which is very costly.

Quiz 6

1. The following entries appeared in the receivables ledger control account for June. Balance b/f 1st June 7,500 yuan, sales 20,000 yuan, receipts from customers 8,000 yuan, discounts allowed 400 yuan, irrecoverable debts written off 500 yuan. What was the balance on 30th June? (   )

    A. 3,600   B. 19,400   C. 19,600   D. 18,600

2. The following balances have been taken from the trial balance of XYZ. What is the trial balance total on the debit side? Rent paid 1,800 yuan, capital 15,000 yuan, purchases 10,000 yuan, sales 12,000 yuan, wages 5,000 yuan, sundry expenses 1,000 yuan, and cash 9,200 yuan. (   ).

    A. 26,000   B. 29,000   C. 42,000   D. 27,000

3. Which of the following is an example of an error of commission (a control account is not kept)? (   ).

    A. A receipt of 25 yuan from J. Gee entered in G. Jay's account as a credit and debited to cash

    B. A purchase of cleaning materials recorded as DR cash 50 yuan, CR cleaning materials 50 yuan

    C. An invoice for 1,300 yuan is lost and not recorded at all

    D. An invoice for 2,500 yuan sales is posted as 2,050 yuan

4. The following entries appeared in the payables ledger control account for February. Balance b/f 1st February 1,700 yuan, purchases 18,000 yuan, paid to suppliers 10,000 yuan, discount received 1,200 yuan, purchase returns 3,000 yuan. What was the balance on 28th February? (   ).

A. 5,500 yuan   B. 2,100 yuan   C. 11,500 yuan   D. 7,900 yuan

5. Which of the following errors would be a possible reason for a trial balance failling to agree? (   ).

    A. Sales 500 yuan entered correctly, but entered as 1,500 yuan in the receivables ledger control account

    B. A purchase of 550 yuan on credit not being recorded

    C. Cash wages being recorded as debit: cash 250 yuan, credit: wages 250 yuan

    D. A non-current asset purchase 750 yuan being recorded as debit: machinery repairs 750, credit: cash 750

6. Which of the following items will appear as an item posted to the payables ledger control account? (   ).

    A. Irrecoverable debts written off

    B. Returns inwards of the period

    C. Discounts allowed in total in the period

    D. Discounts received in total in the period

7. A business maintains a receivables ledger control account. A debt of 1,500 yuan is to be written off. Which of the following entries is correct (ignoring sales tax)? (   ).

    A. Debit: Personal account of the customer, credit: Irrecoverable debts expense

    B. Debit: Irrecoverable debts expense, credit: Receivables ledger control

    C. Debit: Receivables ledger control account, credit: Irrecoverable debts expense

    D. Debit: Irrecoverable debts expense, credit: Personal account of the customer

8. Which of the following is an unlikely reason for a disagreement between a receivables ledger control account balance and the total of balances from the receivables ledger? (   ).

    A. A page in the sales daybook has been incorrectly added

    B. There could be an omission of a balance from the total of the list of balances

    C. An invoice has not been entered in the sales daybook

    D. The control account balance has been incorrectly calculated

9. An error of principle would occur if (   ).

    A. plant and machinery purchased was credited to an non-current assets account

    B. plant and machinery purchased was debited to the purchase account

    C. plant and machinery purchased was debited to the equipment account

    D. plant and machinery purchased was debited to the correct account but with the wrong amount

10. A suspense account shows a credit balance of 130 yuan. This could be due to (   ).

    A. omitting a sale of 130 yuan from the receivables ledger

    B. recording a purchase of 130 yuan twice in the purchases account

    C. falling to write off an irrecoverable debt of 130 yuan

    D. recording an electricity bill paid of 65 yuan by debiting the bank account and crediting the electricity account

11. If a purchase return of 48 yuan has been wrongly posted to the debit of the sales returns account, but has been correctly entered in the supplier's account, the total of the trial balance would show (　　).

　　A. the credit side to be 48 yuan more than the debit side

　　B. the debit side to be 48 yuan more than the credit side

　　C. the credit side to be 96 yuan more than the debit side

　　D. the debit side to be 96 yuan more than the credit side

12. Which of the following correctly describes the function of a credit sales invoice which a customer has received from the supplier? (　　).

　　A. It is a receipt for money paid

　　B. It is a demand for immediate payment by the supplier

　　C. It is a record of goods purchased by the customer

　　D. It is a demand for payment within an agreed time from the supplier

13. Which of the following correctly describes the function of a credit note issued by a supplier to one of its customers? (　　).

　　A. A demand for payment

　　B. An agreed allowance which can be deducted from the next invoice payment

　　C. A loan available to the customer

　　D. A document used by the supplier to cancel part or all of a previously issued invoice

14. Which of the following correctly describes the term "debit term"? (　　).

　　A. It is issued by a supplier to a customer to demand payment in full for goods supplied

　　B. It is issued by a customer to a suppler to request a credit note

　　C. It is issued by a customer when goods are delivered

　　D. It is issued by a customer to a supplier to cancel an invoice received.

15. Which of the following correctly explains the term "trade discount"? (　　).

　　A. A reduction in the amount of an invoice which a customer will pay

　　B. A price reduction which a supplier agrees with all customers in a particular trade

　　C. A price reduction which a supplier agrees with an individual customer after an invoice has been sent at full price

　　D. A reduction in the invoice price by a supplier because of the nature of the business with an individual customer

16. Which of the following statements is correct? (　　).

　　A. Output tax charged to a customer is debited to the sales tax account

　　B. A machine is purchased for 200 yuan plus sales tax 35 yuan. The machinery account is debited with 200 yuan and the sales tax account debited with 35 yuan, the sales tax is irrecoverable

　　C. If the sales tax account has a debit balance at the end of the sales tax quarter, the balance is recoverable from the government

    D. The sales figure in the income statement of a sales tax registered business includes sales tax

17. Accounts are classified according to the nature of the transactions which are recorded in them. Which of the following classifications is incorrect? (   ).

    A. Insurance is recorded in a nominal ledger account

    B. Rents received are recorded in a nominal ledger account

    C. Sales transactions with individual customers are recorded in a personal ledger

    D. Control accounts are kept in the personal ledger

18. Which of the following statements best explains the term "memorandum account"? (   ).

    A. One used for the correction of errors

    B. One used to record transactions between the business and its proprietor

    C. An account used to record information, which does not form part of the double entry system

    D. An account used to summaries transactions before they are posted to the ledgers

19. A machine (cost 5,000 yuan) is bought on credit from X company. Subsequently, 1,000 yuan of the debt to X company is paid by cheque. Which of the following correctly records the transactions? (   ).

    A. Debit X 5,000, credit Machine 5,000. debit Bank 1,000, credit X 1,000

    B. Debit X 5,000, credit Machine 5,000. debit X 1,000, credit bank 1,000

    C. Debit Machine 5,000, credit X 5,000, debit Bank 1,000, credit X 1,000

    D. Debit Machine 5,000, credit X 5,000, debit X 1,000, credit Bank 1,000

20. What is the total of a discounts allowed column in a cash book (assuming a control account is kept)? (   ).

    A. Credited to discounts allowed and debited to sales

    B. Debited to sales and credited to cash

    C. Debited to discount allowed and credited to receivables ledger control account.

    D. Debited to cash and credited to sales

21. A firm keeps an analyzed cash book containing discount received and allowed columns. At the end of an accounting period discounts received totaled 525 yuan and discounts allowed 326 yuan. Which of the following correctly shows the treatment of theses totals? (   ).

    A. Debit discount received 525 yuan, credit discount allowed 326 yuan

    B. Debit discount allowed 525 yuan, credit discount received 326 yuan

    C. Credit discount received 199 yuan

    D. Debit discount allowed 326 yuan, credit discount received 525 yuan.

22. Which prime entry record are returns outwards recorded in? (   ).

    A. Sales returns daybook   B. The journal

    C. The cash book   D. The purchase returns daybook

23. Which prime entry record are credit notes sent out recorded in? (   ).

A. Sales returns daybook   B. Nominal ledger

C. Sales day book   D. Purchase returns daybook

24. Which of the following should appear on the credit side of a suppliers account in the payable ledger? (   ).

A. Payments made   B. Discounts allowed

C. Discounts received   D. Purchase invoices received

25. Calculate the gross pay of an employee who received a guarantee minimum wage of 50yuan per week and who works on a piece work system where output is paid at 10 yuan per unit. Time worked in excess of 40 hours is paid at 3 yuan per hour. In a given week the employee produced 7 units and worked for 45 hours. (   ).

A. 85 yuan   B. 65 yuan   C. 70 yuan   D. 135 yuan